In Two Minds

A Thriller

Richard Harris

A Samuel French Acting Edition

SAMUELFRENCH-LONDON.CO.UK
SAMUELFRENCH.COM

Copyright © 2002 by Wishbone Ltd
All Rights Reserved

IN TWO MINDS is fully protected under the copyright laws of the British Commonwealth, including Canada, the United States of America, and all other countries of the Copyright Union. All rights, including professional and amateur stage productions, recitation, lecturing, public reading, motion picture, radio broadcasting, television and the rights of translation into foreign languages are strictly reserved.

ISBN 978-0-573-01968-5

www.samuelfrench-london.co.uk

www.samuelfrench.com

FOR AMATEUR PRODUCTION ENQUIRIES

UNITED KINGDOM AND WORLD
EXCLUDING NORTH AMERICA
plays@SamuelFrench-London.co.uk
020 7255 4302/01

Each title is subject to availability from Samuel French,
depending upon country of performance.

CAUTION: Professional and amateur producers are hereby warned that *IN TWO MINDS* is subject to a licensing fee. Publication of this play does not imply availability for performance. Both amateurs and professionals considering a production are strongly advised to apply to the appropriate agent before starting rehearsals, advertising, or booking a theatre. A licensing fee must be paid whether the title is presented for charity or gain and whether or not admission is charged.

The professional rights in this play are controlled by The Agency Ltd, 24 Pottery Lane, Holland Park, London W11 4lZ.

No one shall make any changes in this title for the purpose of production. No part of this book may be reproduced, stored in a retrieval system, or transmitted in any form, by any means, now known or yet to be invented, including mechanical, electronic, photocopying, recording, videotaping, or otherwise, without the prior written permission of the publisher. No one shall upload this title, or part of this title, to any social media websites.

The right of Richard Harris to be identified as author of this work has been asserted by him in accordance with Section 77 of the Copyright, Designs and Patents Act 1988

IN TWO MINDS

First presented by Bill Kenwright at the Theatre Royal. Windsor on 5th June 2001 with the following cast :

David Freedman	Marc Bannerman
Annie Bishop	Helen Grace
Anthony Hewlett	Garfield Morgan
Gina	Angela Simpson

The play was directed by **Bob Tomson**
Designed by **Julie Godfrey**
Lighting by **Nick Richings**

CHARACTERS

David Freedman, very negative, late 30s
Annie Bishop, very positive, mid 30s
Anthony Hewlett, tight, proper, 70s
Gina, sparky, bright, a cleaner, late 20s

The action takes place in the sitting room, hallway and kitchen/breakfast room of a Victorian semi-detached corner house in outer London.

Time: the present. A few weeks in late summer

SYNOPSIS OF SCENES

ACT I

Scene 1	The sitting-room and hallway. Early afternoon in late summer
Scene 2	The kitchen/breakfast room. A few days later. Afternoon
Scene 3	The sitting-room and hallway. The next day. Early afternoon
Scene 4	The kitchen/breakfast room. The following Monday. Morning
Scene 5	The sitting-room and hallway. The same day. Late evening
Scene 6	The kitchen/breakfast room. The following Friday. Morning
Scene 7	The sitting-room and hallway. The same evening

ACT II

Scene 1	The kitchen/breakfast room. The following Monday. Mid-morning
Scene 2	The sitting-room and hallway. Next day. Late afternoon
Scene 3	The kitchen/breakfast room. The following Friday. Morning
Scene 4	The sitting-room and hallway. The next morning
Scene 5	The kitchen/breakfast room. The following Monday. Morning
Scene 6	The sitting-room and hallway. Two days later. Evening
Scene 7	The kitchen/breakfast room. Immediately following
Scene 8	The sitting-room and hallway. The next day. Late morning

SETTING

For the purposes of this Acting Edition it is assumed that the play will be performed without a revolve showing the two locations. Rather the set is seen as though the outer wall of the house, towards the audience, has been sliced off so that we see stage right the bay window of the sitting-room, then the two "knocked-though" rooms with the hall and front door to the rear of the stage, and stage left is the kitchen/breakfast room with the french windows to the garden at extreme stage left. The Lighting Plot reflects the change of lighting emphasis from stage right to stage left, although the setting can be achieved in other ways, such as the audience being positioned "in the garden" and front or back stage being lit for the action in either sitting-room/hall or kitchen/breakfast room.

ACT I

Scene 1

The tastefully-decorated sitting-room and hallway of a Victorian semi-detached corner house in outer London. Early afternoon, late summer

The glazed front door is slightly ajar. The sitting-room comprises the two ground floor rooms knocked into one

The previous occupants have recently moved out, so that the rooms are bare apart from carpet and curtains which are part-drawn across two of the three windows that make up the bay, and a large sofa. Beneath the windows is a boxed-in radiator, the top of which serves as a window seat. There are copious empty book shelves. Marks where pictures were hung. The original marble fireplaces. Two windows between the fireplaces. A couple of cardboard boxes containing books and ornaments. Three paintings stacked against a wall. A telephone on the floor. In the hallway is a long, similarly boxed-in, radiator, the top of which serves as a shelf, with three or four letters on it

At rise of CURTAIN, *David enters through the front door, carrying a cardboard box full of more odds and ends. He pushes the door shut with his behind and carries the box through into the sitting-room. He sets the box down with the others and starts drawing back one of the curtains*

Annie enters from the kitchen, carrying a bottle of champagne and two glasses

Annie Look what I found. (*She indicates the bottle and glasses*)
David Where was that?
Annie In the fridge. He left it for us, glasses and all, wasn't that nice of him?
David Very.

She holds out the bottle

Annie Right then.
David Now?
Annie Of course now.

He hesitates

David Let me just move the car.
Annie Why?
David Well, I can't leave it sticking out like that, can I?
Annie Sod the car—open the champagne.
David Annie...
Annie Oh, come on, David, it's a special day for us, don't spoil it.

Again he hesitates, but then smiles, takes the bottle from her

David (*opening the bottle*) What made you look in the fridge?
Annie I don't know: I just opened the fridge and there it was.
David Always assuming he left it for us, of course.
Annie (*lightly*) God, you're so predictable. "Always assuming he left it for us". Who else would he leave it for?
David I was joking.
Annie Oh, yes?
David (*grinning*) Sort of.
Annie He left a note. (*She puts the glasses on the window seat and takes a small piece of paper from her pocket, moving close to him to read, exaggeratedly*) "To my new friends, Annie and David... I know you'll be as happy here as we were... Ike". (*She waves the paper close into his face, wrinkling her nose at Mister Moaner*)

He grins, pulling the cork as she stands the paper up on the mantlepiece. He pours two glasses, giving himself only half a glass, passes the other glass to her. He toasts her, toasts the house

David Like the man says ... happy house.
Annie We will be happy here, David, I know we will.

A moment. He gives a little smile

David Yes. (*He kisses her lightly on the cheek*)

A car horn sounds. Brief but irritable. David looks out of the window

There you are.
Annie What?
David Someone complaining about the car.
Annie Oh dear.

Act I, Scene 1   3

David It will be oh dear if the back gets swiped.
Annie Then move it. Move it, move it, move it. (*She knocks back her champagne*)
David Well ... we're not going to be here long. Are we?
Annie Long enough to finish this. (*She makes to top up his glass*)
David Whoa.
Annie Oh, don't be so boring, David, he left it for us.
David Yes, and very nice of him it was too, but I'm working this afternoon and besides which, I'm driving.
Annie (*brightly*) I'm not. (*She pointedly tops up her glass and toasts him*)

He is forced to take a sip of his drink, but then glances out of the window again

David I wonder if it's always as hard to park as this.
Annie I'm surprised it wasn't on your list of things to ask him.

He looks at her. She pulls a jokey face at him

David I don't have a "list".
Annie You do, you bloody do.
David If I don't write things down, I don't remember.
Annie Poor old soul. (*She mimes a kiss at him*)
David Still. Bound to be, I suppose, with that college up the road. (*He glances out of the window*) I've been thinking: maybe we should get rid of one of the cars. We won't really need two, will we? Not now.
Annie (*firmly*) We will need two cars because I work and I need my car to get there.
David Yes, but...
Annie No, David.
David OK. OK. (*He holds up his hands in mock surrender*)
Annie (*pointedly changing the subject*) Why don't we give him a ring?
David Who?
Annie *Ike.*
David Why?
Annie To say thank you.
David He's in Australia.
Annie So?
David It's the middle of the night.
Annie Oh, yes, I suppose it will be.
David Besides ... the phone probably isn't on.
Annie The electricity's on, the gas is on, so is the telephone.

He nevertheless takes up the receiver and listens briefly

David (*replacing the receiver*) It wouldn't have been if I hadn't kept chasing 'em.
Annie (*not heavily*) You know, you really are impossible.
David I know.

She looks at him, shakes her head slightly and changes the subject

Annie It's not bad, you know. This carpet. It's not bad at all. (*She vaguely scuffs it with the toe of her shoe*) I mean, I'm not mad about the colour but at least it's neutral and it'll certainly do until we can afford to replace it. God, think what it's saving us.
David I do. (*He kisses her lightly*) Sorry.

She returns the kiss

Annie I so like this room. It's got such a—good feel. The whole house. Oh, I know it'll take time to——
David (*suddenly*) Annie, you don't think we've made a mistake, do you? You don't think we've rushed into it, buying this house. I mean, we never think very far ahead, do we, either of us—and sometimes I worry that I, well, I've ... pushed you into it.

A moment. She moves to him, cups his face in her hands, kisses him. Then embraces him, so that they are not looking at each other

Annie I love you. I want to be with you. You know that.
David Sometimes I just need to hear you say it.
Annie You're a funny little man at times.
David (*grinning*) Thanks.
Annie You need so much reassurance, don't you?
David I just ... well... I've made so many mistakes, I suppose.
Annie Who *hasn't* made mistakes? Who?
David Yeah. Yeah, I suppose so.
Annie We're going to be happy here, I know we are. But we're going to have to work at it. Both of us. We're going to have to put the past in its proper place. Aren't we?

A moment

David Yeah. (*He squeezes her, kisses her brow. Brightly*) So, then. What are we supposed to be doing?
Annie Measuring the front bedroom for new curtains.
David Measuring the front bedroom for new curtains. Gotcha. (*He makes to move away*)

Annie Only not right now. (*She pointedly draws the curtain that he had earlier pulled back, goes to him, kisses him*)

The embrace becomes more passionate and they move first to the sofa and then to the floor, caressing and undressing each other in the shadows

The front door opens and Hewlett enters, taking a key from the front door

He closes the door and moves in but stops, seeing the letters on the radiator shelf. Which surprises him slightly. He glances at them, sees they are all junk mail and nothing of significance and is about to go out again

On second thoughts, Hewlett closes the door and, still holding the envelopes, moves along the hallway, past the stairs, and out of sight into the kitchen

Hearing the sound of the front door being pushed shut, Annie and David react … who the hell is that? They scramble to dress themselves, Annie remaining on the floor DS *of the sofa as David moves closer to the door*

David (*calling tentatively*) Hallo?

They wait. Then David motions for Annie to stay where she is and moves cautiously into the hallway

Hewlett enters from the kitchen

The two men come face to face, Hewlett still with the mail and key in his hands

Who the hell are you?

Hewlett, taken totally off-guard, can only stare at him

Well?

Hewlett makes a visible effort to take control

Hewlett Tell me who *you* are and you might get an answer.

David almost laughs at the man's cheek. Annie remains on hands and knees

David I'll tell you who I am—I'm the owner of this house and I want to know what you're doing here.

Hewlett Ah. You're Mr Feldman.
David Freedman, David Freedman—well?

Hewlett doesn't rush to answer

Hewlett My name is Hewlett. I live—(*he indicates the party wall*) next door. I was asked by the previous occupant to collect and forward any mail that might be delivered. (*He holds up the mail, and carefully places it on the shelf*) Had I known you were here I of course would not have presumed to enter unannounced.

Annie—still on hands and knees—puts her head round the sofa so that she is for the first time visible to Hewlett

Good afternoon.

During the following, Annie gets to her feet

David Oh, well, look, umm... I'm pleased to meet you... I'm sorry if, umm... (*He rather awkwardly offers a hand*)

They shake hands briefly

David Freedman, as I say, and this is my... um... this is my partner, Annie. Ann Bishop.

Annie gives Hewlett her friendly smile

Annie Hallo.
Hewlett Hewlett. Anthony Hewlett. (*He gives a formal little tilt of the head*) I'm sorry if I disturbed you.
Annie No no, we were, um, we were just measuring up. (*She has a little fit of laughter—something she's wanted to do since they were caught at it. She recovers quickly*) Won't you, umm, won't you come through?
Hewlett Not if I'm...
Annie No no—please. (*She shoots a little look at David*)
David Please.

A brief moment

Hewlett Thank you. (*He moves into the sitting-room*)

Behind his back David mimes to Annie "Why did you ask him to do that?"

Act I, Scene 1

but she stifles another fit of laughter, indicates to David that one of his shirt buttons is undone and moves into the room where Hewlett stands looking around, making no pretence at hiding his interest in the items they have brought here. During the following, David buttons his shirt and comes in

Annie (*drawing back the curtains; brightly*) Now then—let me offer you a glass of champagne. (*She holds up the bottle*)

Hewlett regards it, unsure

Hewlett Ah. Well, now.
Annie Please—we're christening the new house. Well—*our* new house.
Hewlett In that case ... thank you. A glass of champagne would be most acceptable.
Annie David.
David (*pointedly*) We've only got two glasses.
Annie That's all right—you won't be wanting any more, will you, darling—not driving. (*She gives him her teasing smile*)
David Well, umm ... no, I suppose not.
Annie Then Mister—Hewlett?
Hewlett Hewlett, Anthony Hewlett.
Annie Mr Hewlett can have your glass. Can't he? (*She smiles "sweetly" and holds out David's glass*)

He takes it

David I'll, umm... I'll give it a rinse.

David nods, "smiles" at Hewlett and goes out

Annie Ike left a bottle in the fridge—wasn't that nice of him?
Hewlett Yes. Very.

Pause

Annie Do sit down. (*She indicates the sofa*)

He sits on the sofa, she sits on the window seat

Hewlett The champagne wasn't all he left I notice. (*He pats the arm of the sofa*)
Annie He was very generous. He left us quite a lot of things. This ... carpets, curtains ... oven, refrigerator ... all sorts of things.

Hewlett Easier than carting it to the other side of the world, I imagine.
Annie Yes.

A moment

   He seemed quite a character. Ike.
Hewlett A character. Yes.
Annie Did you know him well?
Hewlett We were ... good neighbours, I suppose you'd say. Nothing more than that.

Annie nods, smiles. This looks like being heavy going

Annie Have you lived here long?
Hewlett My wife and I moved here nearly twenty years ago.
Annie (*cheerily, trying to lighten things up*) Twenty years ... you must like it here.
Hewlett My wife died five years ago.
Annie Oh. I'm sorry.
Hewlett Five years next month.

She nods sympathetically. Pause

Annie Do you have, er, do you have a family?
Hewlett You mean children.
Annie Well, yes, I...
Hewlett No. It wasn't possible.

Another pause

Annie So you, umm, you live on your own, do you?

He looks at her as though he doesn't understand the question

   You live on your own.
Hewlett I should have said first wife. I married again.

Annie is not a little relieved to see David coming in, holding the washed glass and a rather ugly beaker which he pointedly holds up to her

Annie Well done.

During the following, David gives Hewlett the glass and pours champagne for all three

Act I, Scene 1   9

We were saying what a character Ike is.
David Yes, yes, he is. Did you tell Mr Hewlett what happened the first time we——
Hewlett The thing is, you see… I was given to understand that you wouldn't be moving in until the end of the month.

David is surprised and irritated at being interrupted

David (*somewhat stiff*) That's true, yes, but Ike said it would be OK for us to start bringing some of our bits and pieces over.
Hewlett And that's all right, is it?
David (*trying to keep it light*) How d'you mean, that's all right?
Hewlett I assume you haven't yet exchanged contracts.
David No. Not yet.
Hewlett Because I've always assumed that until one——
David I'm sorry, perhaps I didn't make myself clear. We had an arrangement.
Hewlett With Mr Elsmore.
David With Ike, yes—sorry—is something worrying you?
Hewlett (*looking at the note on the mantlepiece*) Because the thing about Mr Elsmore—Ike—at least in my experience—is that he is rather inclined to—shall we say—bypass authority and "do his own thing". It can create problems. If not for him, for those with whom he has dealings and who all too often have been left to… clear up the mess. (*He looks directly at David*) That's why I was—concerned.
David Thank you, but it's all been cleared. With the estate agent *and* the solicitor.
Annie Anyway… we're delighted to meet you. (*She looks at David*)
David Yes.

They both raise their glasses to Hewlett who returns the compliment. They drink. Again the awkward pause

Annie Mr Hewlett has lived here for nearly twenty years.
David Oh?

Slight pause

And you're, umm, you're retired, are you?
Hewlett Unfortunately yes.
David (*trying to keep it light*) Not all it's cracked up to be.

Hewlett seems not to understand

Retirement. Although I suppose if you've——

Hewlett What line of business are you in, Mr Freedman?
David Books. I sell books.
Hewlett A bookshop.
David No no. Wholesale. I have my own company. Non-fiction. Textbooks, manuals and so on.
Hewlett (*to Annie*) And you, er...
Annie Annie, please. I'm a physiotherapist.
Hewlett A physiotherapist. Ah.
Annie At St Bernard's.

Hewlett nods

Hewlett Do you have children?
Annie David does. Two.
David One of each.
Annie If you're worried about the noise—they won't be living with us.
David Not all the time, anyway.
Annie That's why we needed somewhere with at least three bedrooms—so that the children could stay.
David And your mother.
Annie And my mother—yes.
David (*to Hewlett*) Annie's at her best with old people, children and animals. (*He grins at Hewlett, all boys together*)

But Hewlett doesn't join in. Instead he points towards the window

Hewlett Is that your car on the corner?
David The Saab, yes.
Hewlett (*getting up and looking out of the window*) I wouldn't make a habit of leaving it like that—they're very hot about that sort of thing round here—you'll find yourself with a ticket. (*He remains looking out of the window*)
David (*stiffly*) Thank you. (*He looks irritably at Annie*)

She grimaces mock-guiltily

Hewlett It was all right until the college started taking all these—overseas students. Every one of them seems to have a car and they park where they like, on the pavement, over peoples' driveways, anywhere they fancy. No consideration at all.
David Just the "overseas students", is it?
Hewlett We did organise a petition and the council or whoever it is started towing them away but it makes no difference, they're back again the next day. More money than sense, obviously.

David grimaces irritably at Annie... "this is terrific"

(*Turning away from the window*) Well then, I mustn't keep you any longer. Thank you for the champagne. (*He gives a tight little smile to Annie*)

It would seem that he has warmed much more to her than to David: something David has not missed

Annie It was lovely to meet you. I hope you and your wife will come in and have a proper drink with us sometime.
Hewlett Yes, that would be, that would be very, err ... will you be coming here again? Before you move in officially?
David Yes, we'll be popping in and out with various bits and pieces. I might even——
Hewlett If I might suggest... I wouldn't leave anything visible. Boxes like this, for example. There's a council estate across the other side of the green and we get a great deal of thieving. An empty house is a prime target. They've only got to look through the window, see something like this—
David Yes. I take your point. Thank you.
Hewlett Knowing that the house is empty I do of course keep my eyes and ears open.
David (*lightly but pointedly*) You didn't see or hear *us* though, did you?

Hewlett looks at him

Hewlett I'm sorry?
David (*less easily*) I said you, umm, you didn't know *we* were in the house.

Hewlett continues to look at David

Hewlett It might be an idea if in future you let me know that you're coming. So that if I hear anything I'll know it's not someone who shouldn't be here.
David Umm, yes, fine, we'll give you a——
Hewlett (*taking out a neat little pad and pen*) It might be better if you telephoned me in advance—I'll give you my number. (*He writes his number, tearing off the sheet and handing it to David*)
David Nine three two eight. Thank you. I'll call you next time we come over. Probably some time tomorrow.
Annie No, not tomorrow, David, you're seeing that man from Sweden.
David Yes, you're right. Just as well you reminded me—as a matter of fact I was——
Hewlett Whenever then. You'll make sure you telephone me.

Annie Yes. Yes, of course.

She smiles, anxious to cover for David's clear irritation at the way Hewlett interrupts him all the time

Hewlett And if there's anything I can do for you, please let me know.
Annie That's very kind. Thank you. Anthony.

A moment. Then Hewlett gives her his polite nod and moves out into the hallway. David and Annie follow him

David Incidentally ... there'll be no need for you to forward the mail. I'll do it.
Hewlett You have the address, do you?
David Yes, I've got the address.
Hewlett Well, then... I suppose it will be all right. Although he did ask *me* to——
David Yes, I'm surprised he didn't make an arrangement with the post office.
Hewlett I imagine it slipped his mind.
David He asked *you* though, didn't he?
Hewlett I'm sorry?
David He asked *you*. To look after the mail.

A slight moment

Hewlett It was very much a last minute thing. He put a note through my door just before he left for the airport.
David Oh. Oh, I see. Well ... as I say ... we'll look after it from now on... (*He opens the front door*) Goodbye, Mr Hewlett.
Annie Bye.

Hewlett turns and looks at her. For a moment it looks as if he is about to say something. Then he gives his nod and goes out

David gives him a sort of wave-off and then closes the door. Annie puts her hand over her mouth to stifle laughter. They move back into the sitting-room

David I don't know what's so funny.
Annie Can you imagine if he'd arrived five minutes later and walked in here and——
David Oh, that's funny, is it?
Annie Well, isn't it?

He glances from the window

David Bloody cheek of the man.
Annie Oh, come on, David, he didn't know we were here, did he?
David So he says.
Annie Don't be so daft.
David Well, it's bloody strange, isn't it—the first time we're here, *he* walks through the door. And what happens? You ask him to stay for a drink. I could have crowned you.
Annie I was being nice to him.
David I know you were being nice to him.
Annie Like you said—thanks very much by the way—old people, kids and dogs. (*But*) We're going to be neighbours.
David Well, if the last ten minutes is anything to go by, I'm really looking forward to it. Did you notice the way he kept interrupting me? Bloody charming, that was.
Annie I think he'd had a couple. Didn't you smell his breath? Whisky, I think.
David And the way he was looking round the place—like we weren't here.
Annie Yes, that was a bit——
David I mean, all right, I can accept that he didn't know we were here ... but it was his whole attitude ... snotty bugger.
Annie Yes, well, he was bound to put your nose out of joint, wasn't he? All that stuff about "overseas students" and "council estates". Right up your street. Darling. (*She gives him a great big smile*)

He looks at her, gives a sardonic little jerk of the head and starts moving the boxes and so on out of sight from the windows. She moves to sit on the window seat, watches him for a moment

You nearly told him we were married, didn't you?
David When?
Annie (*exaggeratedly*) "And this is my, um, this is my partner, Annie".
David Yes, I did, didn't I? Don't know why. Someone like him, it's just easier, I suppose.
Annie You don't know him.
David (*lightly*) Oh, come on, Annie, you said yourself, you only had to listen to him. He's so bloody proper I bet he wears an elastoplast over his arse.

She watches him move another box and smiles to herself

Annie You find that really hard to say, don't you? "My partner".
David Yeah. I suppose I do.
Annie And you go on about *him*.

David I'd like to marry you—yes.
Annie When we're ready.
David Over a year and we're not ready.
Annie We don't *have* to get married, David, we really don't.

A moment. Then, still holding a box, he kisses her lightly

David No. (*He puts the box down with the others*) He's still got our key.
Annie We should have asked him for it.
David He should have given it to us.
Annie Oh, well … we'll knock and ask him for it when we go.
David No, that'll look a bit off… I'll get it next time we're over.

A moment

Annie I suppose we'd better go up and do the curtains.
David Yeah.
Annie Unless…
David (*kissing her brow*) Come on, Ada … curtains. (*He goes into the hallway*)

She knocks back the last of her champagne and moves through after him

Annie I must give the cleaner a ring.
David Let's hope she's any good.
Annie Ike said she was terrific. Have you got the tape measure?
David (*automatically patting his pockets*) Shit.

She pats his cheek and moves past him and starts up the stairs

  If he was here collecting the mail, why was he in the kitchen?
Annie Why was he what?
David He was coming out of the kitchen.
Annie Are you sure?
David I saw him.
Annie I dunno … he said there've been a lot of break-ins, I suppose he was just checking that everything was all right.

A moment

David Yeah.

  Annie continues up the stairs

Act I, Scene 2   15

David goes back into the sitting-room and looks around briefly and goes out into the hallway

(*Calling up the stairs*) I must have left it in the car! (*He goes towards the front door, but catches sight of the mail on the radiator shelf. He takes it up, considers. Oh well. He tosses down the mail*)

David goes out of the front door, leaving it ajar

And we hold this moment of the empty room. Silent for a moment. And then we hear, and growing louder, the ticking of a grandfather clock

Scene 2

The kitchen/breakfast room. A few days later. Afternoon

This is a large converted room with french doors leading out into the rear garden. A door—open at the moment—leads into a walk-in cupboard. They haven't moved in yet—there are some unpacked boxes. A cordless telephone is to one side

Annie and Gina sit, drinking coffee from mugs, at the worktop which divides the two areas. Gina is very relaxed, at home, sure of who she is. She always wears a thin gold necklace

Annie What did you do for the Elsmores?
Gina Three times a week. Monday, Wednesday and Friday.
Annie I'd only want you twice a week.
Gina Suits me—I've got another lady wants me on the Wednesday.
Annie Say Monday and Friday then.
Gina Monday and Friday.
Annie What about money?
Gina Same as I got from the Elsmores.
Annie Right. Well then, I'm happy if you are.
Gina We'll give it a go then: see how we like each other.
Annie When could you start?
Gina Sooner the better as far as I'm concerned.
Annie Well, we don't officially move in until the 27th—next Friday.
Gina So why don't I start the Monday after?
Annie Great.
Gina Monday after next, nine o'clock.
Annie Nine o'clock—great. (*She smiles*) Thank God that's over—how about another coffee?

Slight pause

Gina Yeah. All right.

During the following, Annie makes two mugs of instant coffee for them

Annie We're very lucky you're still available.
Gina Ike said about now. If I hadn't heard from you by the end of the week I was starting at this other house.
Annie How long were you with them—the Elsmores?
Gina About—eighteen months. Something like that.
Annie We only ever met *him*. Ike. His wife had already gone back to Australia.
Gina You didn't miss anything.
Annie I take it you didn't like her.
Gina No, I didn't. I liked *him*. Ike. He was a very kind man. Once I was having a really bad time and he was—very kind.
Annie We couldn't quite figure out what sort of work he was in. Something about import export I think he said—he wasn't very clear. (*She gives Gina a mug of coffee*)
Gina Ta. He was into all sorts of ducking and diving. A trader I heard him call himself on the phone. He turned the back bedroom into his office—well, you should have seen it. Whatever he did he made a living out of it. Enough to keep madam happy, anyway.
Annie He was also a bit of a do-it-yourself man by the look of it.
Gina Oh, yeah, he loved all that. He said it was therapeutic. Like he'd bring home a load of wood and a bucket o' nails and two days later you'd have thirty shelves and a wardrobe.

Annie smiles. A moment

Annie So. We're just going to move in and change things as and when we feel like it.
Gina Best way, innit? Then you can forget all about it.
Annie It was wonderful. He left us the fridge, oven, all sorts of things. Just left them. The oven's nearly new.
Gina Yeah, I remember when he got it. One of his "deals".
Annie Why did they go back, any idea?
Gina Because she wanted to. She didn't like it here.
David (*off; calling*) Hallo!
Annie In here!

David comes in, carrying a box full of bits and pieces

Act I, Scene 2   17

David (*seeing Gina*) Oh ... hallo.
Annie This is Gina—you remember, I said she was coming.
David Oh—yes—of course. Hallo, Gina, nice to meet you.
Gina How d'you do?
Annie This is David.

David kisses Annie lightly

David (*taking the box into the cupboard*) All sorted?
Annie She's starting the Monday after we move in.
David (*from the cupboard*) Great.
Annie (*lightly*) And she'll have a lot to do so stay out of her way.
David (*coming out of the cupboard and grinning at Gina*) Me?
Annie No nonsense, Gina—if he gets under your feet, give him a wallop.
Gina You work at home as well, do you?
Annie No, he doesn't, but he goes to the office when he feels like it.
David I can speak for myself, thank you. No, I don't, but I go to the office when I feel like it.
Annie All right for some.
David Ah—yes—well—it's not *quite* like that.
Annie Tell you what—just in case—we should give you a key.
Gina Yeah, the Elsmores gave me a key.
David I'll get one cut. Damn cheek, I shouldn't *have* to.
Annie We're having a bit of trouble with next door.
David A bit?
Annie Ike gave him a key to keep an eye on the place and we can't get it back.
Gina Yeah, he can be a funny old devil, the Colonel.
David Colonel?
Gina He was in the army. People call him the Colonel.
David The army. He would be.
Gina I think it was Ike who started it. It appealed to his sense of humour: him being brought up with aborigines and having a colonel to do the garden.
Annie How d'you mean, do the garden?
Gina Ike hated gardening—the one thing he wouldn't turn his hand to—and she hated anything if it got her nails dirty so the colonel used to do it for 'em. I don't think they paid him, he just liked doing it. Or maybe they did. I dunno. Anyway. Something to do, I suppose, poor old sod.
David Colonel.
Annie I quite like him.
David Annie's trouble is she always sees the best in people. Except me.
Gina Sad.
Annie What's she like, his wife?
David "The Colonel's lady".

Gina Not for me to say, is it?
David Hallo—a whiff of scandal.
Gina Dunno about scandal.
David What's she like then?
Annie Stop being an old woman.
David Gossip—I love it. Come on, Gina, what's she like?
Gina I must go, I've got to pick the kids up. Monday week then, nine o'clock. Bye.
Annie I'll see you to the door.
Gina No no, don't bother—bye.
David Bye.

Gina goes out

David realizes he hasn't made his coffee and starts making one

Annie Well. She seems nice—I think we're very lucky.
David So do I. (*He kisses her briefly on the mouth*) I'm starving.
Annie So am I—have you got anything else to bring in?
David Just some books and stuff—why don't we try that Indian next to the station?
Annie Good idea.

David drinks his coffee as Annie rinses the two mugs

   She was telling me how good he was to her.
David Who?
Annie Ike.
David Oh, yeah?
Annie How much she liked him.
David So did you.
Annie Yes, I did.
David Fancied him more like.
Annie Yes, all right—I fancied him.
David Charming.
Annie If you don't want an answer, don't ask the question.
David I'll bring that stuff in.
Annie D'you want a hand?
David No no—you have a lie down and dream about other men.
Annie So what's new?

He makes to go out but stops

David Are you sure about giving her a key?

Act I, Scene 2   19

Annie Why shouldn't we?
David Because we don't know her.
Annie Ike said she was totally trustworthy.
David Oh, well, as long as Ike said so—have we got any potatoes?
Annie Potatoes? Why?
David Because that same selfish bugger's parked right up against you again—there's no way you're going to get out.
Annie So?
David So if I shove a potato up his exhaust it'll fuck up his engine.
Annie I don't believe this.
David Not permanently, just enough to——
Annie Tell me you don't mean it.
David Annie—he's a selfish——
Annie Tell me you don't mean it.
David (*grinning*) I don't mean it. Yes, I do. No, I don't.

David goes out, still arguing with himself deliberately loudly so that she can hear

Annie stands for a moment. Then starts unpacking the box he brought in. As she does, the phone rings close to her, causing her to start a little. She answers it

Annie (*into the phone*) Hallo? (*The caller doesn't answer*) Hallo? (*Again no answer and so she switches off the phone. She stands for a moment, and then dials 1471 then 3*) Hallo? Anthony? ... It's Annie from next door—did you phone just now? ... Oh, I see. ... No, no, not at all, I've made the same mistake myself. ... Absolutely. Bye. (*She switches off the phone. Not quite convinced by his explanation*)
David (*off; calling*) I'll leave it in here.
Annie (*going to the door*) Sorry?
David (*off; calling*) I'm putting it in the sitting-room.
Annie Oh—yes—right.
David (*off*) Who was that on the phone?

A moment

Annie Wrong number. (*She goes back to taking stuff from the box*)

SCENE 3

The sitting-room and hallway. The next day. Early afternoon

There is now a small Edwardian cushioned chair, a couple of table lamps, some books on the shelves. Most of the pictures have been hung

David stands on some low steps hanging a picture

After a moment, the front door opens and Annie enters with some minimal food shopping

David Hallo?
Annie Hi. (*She comes into the room*) You're early.
David I thought I'd hang these pictures. What d'you think?
Annie Nice.

Annie goes straight out and along to the kitchen

David (*calling after her*) What d'you mean, nice, you haven't looked.
Annie (*off, calling*) Sorry?
David (*calling*) I said … it doesn't matter.
Annie (*off*) Sorry?
David (*calling*) I said you haven't looked.

Annie comes back into the room, minus the shopping, and plonks herself on to the sofa

Annie Looked at what?

He can never be sure if she's teasing him

David The paintings.
Annie Oh, the *paintings*. (*She surveys his work*) Very nice.

He checks the level of the picture

> I know what he means about the cars. I had to park halfway down the street. Down a bit on the left.

David Are you sure?
Annie Absolutely.
David (*adjusting the picture*) I ordered the papers.
Annie Oh, good.

Act I, Scene 3

David Start next week.
Annie (*of the painting*) That's it—stop.
David Mmm. (*He's clearly unsure. He makes to take up another picture*)
Annie Oh, don't do any more. David, come and talk to me.

He sits next to her, an arm around her back, kisses her brow. They sit in silence for a moment

David He was quite a little mine of information.
Annie Who?
David Bloke in the paper shop. Mr Shivraj.
Annie Like what?
David Like for example... Ike never paid his paper bill.
Annie Wowee.
David (*grinning*) And—and—he used to order a porno mag.
Annie The little tinker.

Slight pause

What else did he tell you?
David The only decent butchers is the one next to Barclays Bank...
Annie Right.
David The only decent fruit and veg is the one opposite the church...
Annie Right.
David And the only decent baker closed down a month ago.
Annie That's really useful. Really really useful.

Slight pause

David He was telling me about next door.
Annie You mean you were asking him about next door.
David No, he was telling me. About the wife.
Annie What d'you mean—"the wife".
David Sorry. His wife. The Colonel.
Annie You're not going to call him that?
David I might.
Annie What about his wife?
David Well, apparently she's about half his age.
Annie And?
David And she's all tits, arse and eye shadow.
Annie (*with an edge*) What d'you mean, tits, arse and eye shadow?
David You know. In your face.
Annie Right up your street, then. (*She clearly doesn't like the way the conversation has been going*)

David I'm only telling you what the man said, Annie.
Annie That he's got a wife who's half his age and in your face? So what?
David So it's not what you'd expect. Is it? Is it? I mean, for chrissake, that's all I'm saying, Annie...
Annie It's just... (*But she decides not to pursue it*)
David Just what?
Annie It doesn't matter. It really doesn't matter. (*She kisses him*) D'you fancy a cup of tea?
David I'll make it.
Annie Only if you want one.
David Don't you?
Annie Not really.
David What about a glass of wine?
Annie Later maybe.

They remain like this, his arm around her

David Have you been burning stuff in the garden?
Annie Here?
David Mmm.
Annie No.
David There's some stuff been burnt in the garden.
Annie Our garden?
David Mmm.

Annie gets up and looks out of the window

Annie Where?
David In that incinerator thing—down the end.
Annie Since yesterday, you mean?
David I dunno: but it wasn't like it when we first came.

The outline of a figure appears at the front door and the doorbell rings

(*Lightly*) Who the hell's that? (*He moves into the hallway so that he can see the outline at the door*) It's him, I think. Next door.
Annie (*lightly*) Oh God.
David Are you expecting him?
Annie No—why should I be?

David opens the door

It is Hewlett

Act I, Scene 3

Hewlett Good afternoon.
David (*over-brightly*) Good afternoon—what can I do for you?
Hewlett I thought I ought to tell you that we had the chap from the water company round—about the meters.

Annie moves to the sitting-room door

David I'm sorry, I'm not with you.
Annie Hallo, Anthony—don't stand there—come inside—please.
David Yes, of course, how rude of me. (*He holds open the door wider*)

After a slight hesitation, Hewlett moves inside

Hewlett I don't wish to disturb you.
Annie You're not disturbing us—come and sit down.

They move into the sitting-room. Hewlett looks around

Hewlett You've put some pictures up.
Annie Yes. Please. (*She indicates for him to sit*)

Hewlett sits on the sofa. Annie sits next to him

David You were saying something about—meters, was it?
Hewlett The water meters, yes.
David What water meters?
Hewlett Ah—yes—it was before your time. (*More to Annie than to David*) The whole area is going over to meters. They need to survey each house.
David What if we don't want a meter?
Hewlett There would appear to be no choice. (*He holds out a card for Annie*) They'd like you to give them a ring to say when you'll be here.
David I'm surprised you didn't let them in yourself. (*He's instantly regretting his impulsiveness*)
Hewlett I'm sorry?
David No, no, I was just...
Hewlett You mean because I have a key.
David Well, yes.
Hewlett (*to Annie*) D'you know, it never occurred to me.
Annie Actually, we were wondering when we could have it back.
Hewlett You want it back.
Annie Well, yes, I——
Hewlett I say that because I thought perhaps you might want the same arrangement I had with the Elsmores.

David Which was what?
Hewlett We each gave the other a key. For emergencies.
Annie Sounds a good idea.
David Great. Very "neighbourly".
Hewlett Unless, of course——
Annie No no, I mean... David?
David Why not?
Hewlett I'll let you have one of mine then. Good. Good.
David What—er—what constitutes an emergency—would you say?
Hewlett Not with you—sorry.
David Well—for example—bloke from the water company wants to get into the house, we're not here, you've got the key...
Hewlett I said. It never occurred to me.
David Yes.
Hewlett I was taking a little nap when he called and wasn't thinking as clearly as perhaps I should have been.
David Right. Right.

An awkward little pause which Annie relieves

Annie You were right about the parking. I've had to park miles away.
Hewlett I heard yesterday that there is a move to have residents' parking.
David Great idea. Keep the buggers out. (*He grins broadly*)

But Hewlett's look makes the grin fade

Hewlett You'd be against it, would you, Mr Freedman?
Annie (*warning*) David.
David It just means they'd park somewhere else, doesn't it? Somewhere else would have the problem.
Hewlett And we wouldn't. (*To Annie*) Yes?
Annie (*lightly*) Yes.
David Cars are getting to be like gypsies, aren't they? They arrive, they get moved on, they arrive somewhere else, they get moved on...
Hewlett You didn't answer my question: would you be against parking restrictions?

A moment

David I suppose not. (*Then brightly, almost insolently*) Dear me, how rude of us—would you like a drink?
Hewlett Thank you—no—I must go.
David (*with fake disappointment*) Oh.

Act I, Scene 3   25

Hewlett and Annie stand

Hewlett And you're moving in this Friday.
Annie This Friday, yes.
Hewlett Have you any idea what time?
Annie Well, they promised before lunch but you know what they're like, these people.
David These people.
Hewlett Because what I could do is try and save you a space.
Annie That would be very kind—thank you.
David Thank you.
Annie (*of the card*) And thank you for this, I'll phone them in the morning.

Hewlett nods, smiles at her—he has clearly taken a great liking to her—and moves to the door. David goes with him. During the following, Annie moves to look out of the front window

David By the way ... you haven't by any chance been burning stuff in our garden, have you?

Hewlett looks at him as though he doesn't understand

I know you used to look after the garden for the Elsmores and I wondered if, umm... (*He leaves it hanging in the air*)
Hewlett Yes, I'm so sorry, I should have said. Mr Elsmore asked me to tidy it up for you before you moved in—get rid of the twigs and leaves and so on. Your moving in early rather caught me on the hop. And because rain is forecast I thought I should get on and do it while I could. I hope I haven't...
David No no no—not at all. (*He smiles in victory*)

Hewlett gives a curt little nod and resumes his journey to the front door. David opens the door for him

Hewlett Good afternoon, Mr Freedman. David.
David Good afternoon... Mr Hewlett. Anthony.

Hewlett remains looking at him for a moment, then nods and goes

David remains at the door. Now Annie and David give a little wave, more or less in unison, and David closes the door and moves into the sitting-room as Annie moves away from the window

Annie You really are intent on giving him a bad time, aren't you?

David All that stuff about the bloke from the water company—he could have shoved the number through the letter box but no, he wants to have a nose around. And what about all that bollocks with the key? We're not going to get it back, you know that, don't you?
Annie They had an arrangement. He said.
David Oh, yeah?
Annie A lot of neighbours do the same thing, you know perfectly well.
David I don't trust him.
Annie Oh God, David.
David All right, all right, I know what you think but I don't trust him. There's something about him that's not kosher.
Annie He'd been drinking again, I'll give you that.
David You know what it's like? It's like he's checking up on us.
Annie Then go next door and say you want it back.
David How can I? Now?
Annie That's right, David.
David That's right what?
Annie There's always an excuse.
David Waddaya mean, excuse?
Annie You never face a problem, you always avoid it and then ... brood over it. Blame someone else.
David Thanks. Thanks a lot.
Annie Or better still—go and stick a potato up his exhaust.
David Very funny ho-ho.
Annie David—he's our neighbour. All right, maybe he's a funny old stick in the mud who likes a tipple but we've got to live with him.
David And his wife. (*He grins*)
Annie And his wife.
David I wonder when *she's* going to put in an appearance?
Annie As soon as we're settled in we'll invite them round for a meal and you can give her the benefit of your boyish charm.
David (*not displeased*) Now would I?
Annie Would you ever. You can't resist. Even with Gina when she was here.
David Gina when she was here what?
Annie You put on a performance.
David Who does?
Annie You do, you can't resist it.
David What d'you mean performance?
Annie Mister Cute, that's what I mean.
David So why do you put up with it?
Annie Because it *is* a performance. Or it had better be. (*She kisses him lightly*) Are we going to have a drink here or shall we go home?
David Err ... here. Then I can finish these pictures.

Act I, Scene 3   27

She kisses him again and makes for the door

Annie Funny when you think next Friday this'll be our home. Proper home. Together.
David Yep.

They smile at each other, then she makes to go to the kitchen

It wasn't just twigs and stuff. In the fire. There was some material. Clothing.
Annie What sort of clothing?
David I dunno: most of it had burned through. Women's clothing, I think. There were some shoes.

A moment

Annie I suppose Ike must have left it.
David Been easier to leave it out for the binmen, wouldn't it?
Annie (*not sounding very convinced*) Perhaps he did. And for some reason they didn't take it and so Anthony—burned it.
David (*teasing*) I'll ask him.
Annie (*concerned*) Oh David—don't—please.
David Excuse me, but you just said...
Annie I know, but it's not that important.
David (*grinning*) Whatever you say, madam. (*He takes a picture off the floor and stands holding it, his back to her*)

Annie stands for a moment and then moves down and into the kitchen

David surveys the wall, whistling cheerily under his breath. But, out of the corner of his eye, sees someone passing the front window

For chrissake, what do you want *now*?

The outline of a figure appears in the doorway as David moves out into the hall and towards the door... but a newspaper is shoved through the letterbox and the figure goes out of sight. David stops, gives a little jerk of the head at his misreading of the moment and then pulls the newspaper from the box. He glances at it—it's a free local ad paper. He tosses it on the side and goes back into the sitting-room and resumes his picture-hanging

SCENE 4

The kitchen/breakfast room. The following Monday morning

David and Annie have moved in. There is now a table and chairs. Two cardboard boxes on the table, three empty ones near the french windows. The radio is playing pop music, not loudly

Gina is drying a whole load of crockery she has washed

Annie enters, using the cordless phone

Annie (*into the phone*) What time does she want? Hold on while I look in my diary. (*She switches off the radio. To Gina*) Won't be a second. (*She takes up her shoulder bag, pulls out her work diary and consults it. Into the phone*) I've got a twelve o'clock with Mr Taylor—why don't you try and get hold of him and see if we can swap them around? If not it'll have to be tomorrow. ... About half an hour. ... No, no, I'll phone her myself—thanks, Dawn—bye. (*She switches off the phone and starts to collect her things together*) How're you doing?
Gina Where d'you want the other stuff? (*She indicates the boxes on the table*)
Annie Oh ... on the shelves in the cupboard. Have you had a coffee?
Gina Later maybe.
Annie Well, you know where everything is.
Gina I should do—I put it there.
Annie (*dialling on the phone*) David should be here before you go—I hope he'll have a key for you.
Gina Right.
Annie I'll brain him if he hasn't.
Gina Men, eh?
Annie Oh, well, they do their best. Such as it is.

They exchange a smile. We should sense that there is already a rapport between them. So that Annie can ask

Why didn't you like Mrs Elsmore?
Gina Because in my opinion she was a cow. He was lovely. Ike. Well, I said, didn't I? Different bloke altogether when she wasn't around.
Annie How d'you mean?
Gina Well—on his own he was—well he was *Ike*. Always friendly, wanting a chat—*interested*. Sit down, have a cuppa tea and tell me what's happening in your world, he'd say. Sod off, Ike, I'd say, I've got my work to do. So have I, he'd say, but what's five minutes? He was—so easy.

Act I, Scene 4   29

Annie I know what you mean: we only met him twice and it was like he was an old friend. (*She starts re-dial the phone during the following*)
Gina But when she was here he scarcely opened his mouth. You could tell he was really nervous of her. Gawd knows what she had over him. Something must have gone on, I suppose. I often wondered. Mind you, he loved the ladies. He could be a very naughty boy, our Ike. (*She gives a little smile to herself*)

Annie finds the line is engaged—decides not to bother and puts the phone down

Annie I know what I meant to ask you: I can sometimes hear next door's clock ticking. Through the wall. As loudly as if it was in the same room.
Gina Yeah, I know. Funny that, innit? Sometimes you can hear everything— clock, phone ringing. Everything.
Annie Probably means they can hear *us*. Oh gawd.
Gina I hate the sound of a clock ticking. I find it—really creepy.
Annie (*looking at her watch*) Right. I'm off. (*She takes up her bag and diary*) I'll see you on Friday.
Gina Bye.
Annie Bye, Gina. (*She makes to go*)
Gina What d'you want done with all the boxes?
Annie Leave them out for the binmen, I suppose.
Gina They won't take 'em.
Annie Oh... I'll get David to burn them.
Gina Or take 'em to the dump. That's what Ike used to do: take everything to the dump. He loved going there. He said it made him feel all righteous. Like getting his hair cut. You should have seen the stuff he bagged up and took there before he left.

A moment

Annie What sort of stuff?
Gina You know—all the usual rubbish people say they're going to throw away and never do.
Annie You mean like—old clothes and things.
Gina No, no, not old clothes. Clothes was the one thing he never dumped. Clothes he took to the Oxfam shop. If I couldn't get me hands on them first.

A moment, and Annie nods

Annie See you Friday, then.
Gina Yeah, see you Friday.

Annie goes out

Gina takes up one of the boxes from the table and carries it into the cupboard, turning on the light so that the interior of the cupboard lights up. The facing walls are brick and lined with shelving. The third wall is flat. There is a vent to the outside of the house. Gina puts the box on a shelf and comes out of the cupboard. She goes back to her work but becomes aware—as do we—of the sound of the clock from next door. She turns on the radio and turns up the volume of the music. She resumes her work

SCENE 5

The sitting-room and hallway. The same day. Late evening

The curtains are drawn. The only light is from the street lamps shining through the front door

We become aware of the ticking clock. The sound fades as we see and hear David and Annie arriving at the front door and unlocking it

David *(off)* A pound.
Annie *(off)* Fifty.
David *(off)* You haven't got fifty.
Annie *(off)* I will have.

> *They come in. In a jolly mood after a good meal. David moves straight into the sitting-room, switching on lights as he goes*

David Right. Fifty quid.
Annie I don't believe this.
David Fifty quid.
Annie Oh, get on with it, you silly little person.

He takes a dictionary down from the shelves and consults it as she switches on side lights and switches off the overhead light

David We should have left the lights on.
Annie We weren't here.
David That's what I mean. We should get some of those timer things... (*Of the dictionary*) There you go... (*He moves to her, indicating*) Occurred... two Cs and two Rs. Two.
Annie Well, why have some words only got one?

Act I, Scene 5

David Er... (*mock-sneaking a look in the dictionary*) Because this is from the latin.
Annie You didn't know that.
David Of course I knew that. Fifty quid you owe me.
Annie Go boil an egg. (*She collapses on to the sofa*)
David Are you reneging on me?
Annie *I'll* do it if *you* can spell it.
David Huh. (*He returns the dictionary to the shelf and moves to slump next to her*)

They sit for a moment

Annie I'm drunk.
David You're kidding.
Annie I am, I'm drunk.
David You know why, don't you?
David ⎫ (*together*) ⎧ You drink too quickly.
Annie ⎭ ⎩ I drink too quickly.
David You do, though, you slurp it down like lemonade.
Annie D'you know what I'm going to do? I'm going to start smoking, then you'll really have something to moan about. Cigars. I'm going to smoke cigars.
David Bloody good restaurant, though, wasn't it?
Annie It was, it was excellent.

A moment. She snuggles into him

You must be really looking forward to this weekend.
David I am. Yes, I really am.
Annie Have you got any plans?
David Not really. It'll just be nice having them here. Not having to plan things. (*He kisses her head*) Thanks for being so understanding about it.
Annie They're your children.
David Yeah, but ... you have to put up with all her crap. My crap.
Annie It'll get easier.
David Please God.
Annie Of course it will. (*She kisses him briefly*) Get me a glass of water, there's a love.
David Just water?
Annie Please.

He kisses her brow briefly, goes out and makes to move along to the kitchen but stops, frozen in the act of listening

David I can hear it *now*.
Annie Sorry?
David The clock. (*He continues to listen for a moment*) Amazing. Sounds like Big Ben. Boing! Boing! Must be something to do with the way these houses are built. D'you know what we are? We are the victims of a bunch of Victorian cowboys.

David goes into the kitchen where he starts to sing his somewhat raucous version of "Girls Were Made To Love And Kiss"

Annie remains sitting, smiling to herself, and then her face changes, something puzzles her. She gets up and moves towards the bay. She stands, then turns to look into the room

Annie (*puzzled*) David...

The phone rings

(*Calling*) I'll get it!

She takes up the phone as David comes out of the kitchen with a large glass of water

Hallo. Hallo?... Ike! Where are you? (*She cups the receiver and mouths to David—"It's Ike"*) What's the time there?... You're mad. Everything's fine, absolutely fine, we love the house, absolutely love it—how are things with you? (*She listens, smiling*)
David Ask him about next door.

She nods, mouthing "all right, all right" and David remains waiting for her to ask the question

Annie Oh, that's wonderful, I'm so pleased for you.
David Ask him about the key.

She waves him away

Annie Well, it was lovely to hear from you too—and Ike—thanks for the champagne, that was so nice of you. We will. We will. Bye. (*She hangs up*)
David You didn't ask him.
Annie Oh David, how could I? (*She sits. There's clearly something on her mind*)

Act I, Scene 5   33

He takes the water to her. She drinks

David All you had to do was ask him.
Annie It's not that important, surely.

A slight moment

David No. You're right. Of course you are. How was he?
Annie He was fine.
David Must be strange, going back after—what—eight years, did he say?
Annie Eight, I think—yes. (*She sips more water*)
David Are you all right?

She manages a smile

Annie Fine.
David He didn't say anything to...
Annie No, no, of course he didn't. I'm just... David... I didn't draw the curtains.
David Curtains?
Annie When I went out to meet you. I didn't leave any lights on and I didn't draw the curtains.

He looks towards the bay

David Are you sure?

She nods

Oh, Christ.
Annie Perhaps he thought...
David When's all this going to end? What else does he do when we're not here? Well, that's it, I've had enough. (*He takes up the phone, and starts dialling, checking against the note Hewlett left*)
Annie What are you doing?
David I'm phoning him, what does it look like? Nine three two eight.
Annie It's nearly half past ten.
David So?
Annie So ... they might be in bed.
David All the lights were on. Come on, come on...
Annie David—please.
David Mr Hewlett? David Freedman, I'd like a word with you. No, not on the phone if you don't mind, I'd rather see you. Now. Yes, I know that but

... no, that would be fine, thank you. (*He replaces the receiver*) He's coming round.
Annie Oh David.
David This is our house. I want to know what he was doing here.
Annie Yes, I know, it's just ... oh, I don't know.
David And I'm having the key back, arrangement or no arrangement. And just to make sure, I'm changing the locks, I mean it's bloody ridiculous.
Annie You see, you're already losing your temper.
David I am not losing my temper, I'm pissed off.

The front doorbell rings

Annie I'll go. And David—try and do it nicely—please. (*She goes and opens the front door*)

Hewlett is outside

Hallo, Anthony—do come through.

They move into the room

Hewlett Everything *is* all right, is it?
Annie Well, um...
Hewlett They didn't come back, I hope?
Annie I'm sorry, I, er...
Hewlett Isn't that why you called?
David What are you saying—sorry.
Hewlett I left you a note.
Annie Note?
Hewlett On the breakfast room table. Did you not see it?
Annie (*looking at David*) No.
David What does it say—your note?
Hewlett That I would speak to you tomorrow.
David About what?
Hewlett About what had happened.
Annie Anthony ... will you tell us—now—please.

He frowns, as though confused at their lack of understanding

Hewlett I saw this type nosing around—just after eight I think it was—trying to get a look in through the window there... I gave you a ring, no answer, I went out after him, he legged it ... so I came in to check that the kitchen windows were all right. I know these types often operate in pairs, one of

Act I, Scene 5   35

them going in through the back. Everything was all right and so as I say I wrote you a little note.

All of which takes the wind out of their sails

Annie And you—closed the curtains.
Hewlett Yes, I thought——
David Did you call the police?
Hewlett I should have done, I suppose.
David But you didn't.

A moment

Hewlett No, I didn't.
Annie Well, anyway, thank you for——
David It's funny this should have happened because I—er, I've had a letter from the insurance people. The people who are insuring the house. They want me to change all the locks. Apparently it's their policy with someone—moving in. (*He waits, hoping Hewlett might make the connection*) What I'm saying is the key you've got won't be of any use and I'd like it back, please.
Hewlett Point taken. (*He feels for the key in his trouser pocket*)
Annie We'll let you have another one when the locks are changed of course—won't we, David?
David Of course.

Hewlett holds up the key

Hewlett There you are.
David (*much relieved*) Thank you. (*He shows his relief to Annie and is about to pocket the key*) I don't think this is ours.
Hewlett Sorry?
David The key. It isn't ours.
Hewlett Are you sure?
David Of course I'm sure.
Hewlett Let me see. (*He takes the key and examines it carefully*)

David's irritation increases

You're absolutely right. This is *my* spare. How did I manage that?
David (*flat*) I've no idea.
Hewlett Anyway. I said I'd let you have one so here you go. (*He holds the key out*)

David ignores it so Annie takes it

David (*slowly, as though to a child*) I would like you to return our key. Please.
Hewlett You mean now.
Annie Tomorrow will be fine. Won't it, David?

A moment between them

David Absolutely. Abso-bloody-lutely.
Hewlett (*with both hands in his jacket pockets*) Just a minute, just a minute ... there. Knew I had it. (*He holds up a key*)

A moment, and David takes it

David Thank you.
Hewlett There we are then. All done and dusted. Anything else, is there?
David No. No, that's all, thank you.
Hewlett Then I shall bid you goodnight. (*He gives David a curt nod and moves out into the hallway*)

Annie goes with him

   Goodnight, Annie.
Annie Goodnight, Anthony. (*She opens the door*)

   Hewlett gives a very slight nod and goes

She closes the door after him. Stands a moment and then moves back into the sitting-room

   You're so bloody *rude* to him.
David Me?
Annie You are, you're so bloody rude to him.
David This is so typical.
Annie Typical of what?
David Typical of the way you always take the other side.
Annie Oh, not that again—please.
David Annie—he was deliberately winding me up.
Annie What d'you mean—winding you up?
David He knew perfectly well he had this key—he was winding me up.
Annie Why? Why would he do that?
David Because he doesn't like me.
Annie Oh God.

David From the minute I met him—getting my name wrong.
Annie You're not saying...
David Yes.
Annie Aren't you being just a little bit over-sensitive?
David You think I don't know? You think I haven't had enough practice?

Slight pause

Annie I think ... it's your attitude. That's all. I think you've summed him up and you're looking for trouble.
David What I should have done of course is leave it to you.
Annie It wouldn't have gone on this long, I tell you that.
David Then why didn't you do it?
Annie Because I know how much you need to be Mister Masterful.

A moment. It's a dangerous moment for both of them

David I'm going to bed. (*He moves to the door. Quietly*) Every time he comes round, he causes trouble. That's all. That's all.

David goes out and upstairs

Annie remains sitting. Then she gets up to follow him upstairs and make peace. On second thoughts, she goes to the front door and puts the chain on

Then, as Annie climbs the stairs we hear the increasing sound of the ticking clock

Scene 6

The kitchen/breakfast room. The following Friday. Morning

David sits at the table, using a laptop computer, whistling cheerily under his breath. His jacket over his chair, a coffee mug at his elbow

Gina enters, carrying a full wastebasket

Gina All right if I come through?
David Absolutely.

Gina goes out through the garden door and returns a short time later carrying the now empty basket

David has remained tapping at the keyboard, still whistling under his breath

Gina (*rinsing her hands*) Someone's happy.
David (*typing*) I've finally done a deal I've been massaging for weeks.
Gina I can have some more polish then, can I?
David Sorry?
Gina I'll be needing some more polish.

He reaches for a sheet of paper and writes expansively

David You need it, you shall have it.
Gina I wish I'd met you a hundred years ago.
David Polish. What sort?
Gina She'll know.
David You'll know. Anything else?
Gina You could tell her I'm not keen on the stuff she's got for the brass. (*She drifts towards him, drying her hands*)
David (*writing*) Not keen on brass stuff. Right.

She ends up standing close behind him, looking down at the laptop

Gina You understand these things, do you?
David Just about. Enough to get round it.
Gina My boy's obsessed.
David They mostly are.
Gina He's got one in his room. I mean, not like this, I mean—you know. He can be hours at it.
David I've got everything I want in this thing. That's what I meant about not needing to go into the office.

She remains behind him, looking at the laptop. He is much aware of her presence

Gina Right then, I'm off. (*She moves away to hang up the towel*)
David How about money?
Gina I saw Annie before she left.

The phone rings

David Hang on a sec, I've got you a key... (*He takes up the phone*) Four seven four four, hallo? (*He listens, his face changing*) Oh. Good morning. (*He listens, turning away from Gina*) Why? Well, why didn't you ... no no, there's nothing I can do about it, is there? I'm not getting into an argument: you've done what you wanted to and that's it. ... You know perfectly well what I mean. I told you: I'm not getting into an argument, I'll speak to you later. (*He rings off sharply*) Cow. (*He sits for a moment, clearly distressed, and then realizes that Gina is there*) I'm sorry, I, er ... where were we? Oh—yeah—the key. (*He takes the key from his jacket pocket*) I finally got it back from him. Next door.

She takes it from him

Sorry. That was my wife. Ex-wife. She's changed her mind about my having the kids this weekend. Apparently she—er—she'd forgotten something they had on. He giveth and he taketh away, eh? (*He gives a flat smile*)
Gina D'you want a cup of coffee?
David (*smiling*) No, thanks.

A moment, then she moves to take up the wastebasket

Gina I'll see you Monday.
David Yeah. See you Monday.

A moment

Gina goes out, taking the wastebasket

He remains sitting

Scene 7

The sitting-room and hallway. The same evening

Annie and Hewlett sit side by side on the sofa. She sips red wine, watching, as he sketches on a pad—both of them very enthusiastic

Hewlett Then as a background and to give us some height... I'd suggest a Ceanothus—say "Blue Mound"—like ... so...
Annie When you say "height"...
Hewlett Perhaps six feet or so.
Annie Uh-huh.
Hewlett And then—here—perhaps some lavender...
Annie Oh, yes, I like lavender. In fact I'd like lavender all over the place.
Hewlett Lavender it is, then. (*He finishes his sketch*) There. (*He passes the

sketch to her) What you'd have then, you see, is cover more or less all the year round.
Annie (*looking at the sketch*) I think that would be lovely.
Hewlett Good. Good. (*He takes up his glass of wine and drinks*)

They smile at each other. And the enthusiasm is replaced by a slight awkwardness

I'm very fond of shrubs.
Annie Yes.
Hewlett I see them as, er, good and faithful companions. With us when all the others—the annuals, the perennials—have disappeared. And so many colours and shapes of their own. The leaves. Berries. Even the bark.
Annie (*smiling*) You really love your garden, don't you?
Hewlett Yes, I suppose I do. I certainly can't imagine how I'd exist without it. No no, that's too dramatic. How I'd fill my day.
Annie And your wife? (*She has asked this despite herself*)
Hewlett My wife.
Annie I wondered if it was something you share.
Hewlett No. My wife—enjoys the results. She has—many other things to occupy her. My first wife—Deirdra—was the enthusiast. It was she who—"turned me onto it" as they say. I had no idea of the pleasure it gave.

The front door opens and David enters, carrying a briefcase

Annie (*calling*) David!
David Hallo. (*He is still down from his earlier disappointment*)
Hewlett I think perhaps I should...
Annie Not at all. (*She calls*) We're in here.

David reacts. "We?" And moves into the sitting-room as Annie and Hewlett stand. Annie moves to him and kisses him lightly

I thought you said about nine.
David We finished early. (*He tosses down his case and smiles humourlessly*) What's this then?
Annie Anthony's been planning our garden for us. (*Said in a way that asks him, please don't be unpleasant*)
Hewlett Just a few suggestions.
David Oh, really?
Annie For that bare bit by the wall.
David Oh, the bare bit by the *wall*. (*He sits, deliberately untidily*)
Annie We're having a glass of wine.

Act I, Scene 7

David So I see.
Annie Anthony brought it.
David Ah.
Annie You'll have one, will you?
David Why not?
Annie I'll get you a glass.
David No no, I'll do it. (*He gets up energetically*) Anything else? Nuts? Nibbles? No?

David goes out, looking angrily at her, and goes into the kitchen

Hewlett I really think I should...
Annie I wouldn't hear of it.
Hewlett Forgive me, but he's obviously...
Annie It isn't you, it's ... his children were coming for the weekend and they've had to cancel. It would have been their first time here. He's done out a room for them and everything. He's ... well, he's very disappointed.
Hewlett Yes. I can understand that.
Annie Finish your drink—please.

David returns with a glass. He pours himself a glass, toasts them, and drinks

David Very nice. Very ... round.
Hewlett From Chile.
David So I see.
Hewlett Left me by the previous encumbent.
David The previous encumbent.
Annie Ike.
David Oh... *Ike*.
Hewlett He had several crates of the stuff. One of his deals. His acquisitions. His ability to—acquire was quite—enviable.

There is a silence. David enjoys it

Annie I was thinking ... perhaps you'd like something to eat?
Hewlett I'm sorry?
Annie With your wife being away I thought perhaps...
Hewlett Ah, yes, I see. (*He smiles at her*) You're very kind but I'm quite able to look after myself, thank you.
David That's the army, is it?

Hewlett looks at him

The army. Self-sufficiency and all that.
Hewlett To an extent, I suppose so, yes.
David Ike called you the Colonel, I understand.
Annie David.
David You don't mind, do you, Anthony? I mean say if you do and we'll talk about gardening or...
Hewlett He occasionally referred to me as such, yes.
David Was that your rank or his way of...
Annie Honestly, David.
David I'm interested—really.
Hewlett It was the rank I retired with.
David After—what?
Hewlett After thirty-two years.
David Thirty-two years a soldier. (*He gives a little whistle*)
Hewlett A long time, yes.
David What regiment were you with? Is that right, regiment?
Hewlett The Parachute Regiment.
David (*"impressed"*) The Paras. So presumably you saw some action.
Hewlett Oh, yes.
David Real bang bang stuff.
Hewlett Enough.
David Killing people.
Hewlett Killing people.
David And now gardening.
Hewlett And now gardening.
David Which do you prefer? (*He smiles, amiably*)
Hewlett Tell me: what sort of name is Freedman?
David It's a German sort of name.
Hewlett German.
Annie David's parents came over here in nineteen thirty-something.
David Nineteen thirty-eight.
Hewlett Ah.
David They were Jewish—yes. And so am I. Is that a problem?
Hewlett It's not a problem for me. Is it a problem for you?
David Oh, and incidentally—Annie isn't Jewish. She is a one hundred and ten percent English rose. What you might call the icing on the kike.
Hewlett (*to Annie*) Am I missing something here?
Annie He's being silly.
David You know Jews: when in doubt tell a joke.
Annie (*quietly*) Stop it.
Hewlett What do you think about Israel?
David What do I think about Israel?
Hewlett I take it you have an opinion.

Act I, Scene 7   43

David I'm a Jew, I've got an opinion about everything.
Hewlett So what do you think?
David About what?
Hewlett About Israel.
David I think they've got some very difficult neighbours.

A moment. And Hewlett stands, gives a little nod to Annie and moves towards the door. She makes to go with him but he stops and turns to David

Hewlett My first tour of duty was in Palestine, during the Mandate. Nineteen forty-seven. We weren't very popular, as you can imagine. The local newspaper called us The Gestapo. My sergeant found that particularly hard to take. His name was Freedman and I seem to remember that his family came out of Poland. What was left of them. Sergeant Freedman. Samuel Freedman. That's why I asked. I thought perhaps you might have been related. Stupid of me. (*He gives a little nod and goes out*)

Annie goes out after him. She opens the door

Thank you for your hospitality.
Annie Thank you for your wine. And your advice.

Hewlett smiles and goes out

She closes the door and goes back into the sitting-room, quietly seething. For a moment they don't speak

Does it ever occur to you that he might not like you not because you're Jewish or black or with one eye in the middle of your forehead but because you're you and sometimes, David——
David Just answer me this, will you? Did you invite him in here?
Annie You said you wouldn't be back until nine.
David So?
Annie So... (*Placating*) We were in the garden, talking over the wall, next thing I know he's round here with his notebook and a bottle of wine. He's just ... being nice.

Suddenly there is the sound of a car alarm. Not over-loud but insistent. He gives an "I don't believe it" jerk of the head and moves to look out of the front window

David I knew it... (*He opens the front door*) Get away from there! Bloody kids... (*He moves back, pulling out his car keys*) Bloody great, isn't it?

You've got *him* next door, kids vandalizing your car every day, a street full of people who can barely say hallo to you—just remind me, will you, just remind me—why the hell did we ever move here?
Annie (*quietly*) Because we chose to move here.
David Well, I tell you, it's a nightmare, a bloody nightmare.

David goes out

She sits, looking straight ahead. After a moment, the car alarm stops. A moment's silence. And we bring up the sound of the ticking clock

CURTAIN

ACT II

Scene 1

The kitchen/breakfast room. The following Monday. Mid-morning

Annie and Gina sit, having a coffee. A moment

Annie I don't know whether getting married might not—upset the balance. Christine—his ex—just somehow can't let go. And poor David's as guilty as hell about his kids—guilty as hell about *everything*—and of course she knows what he's like and turns the knife whenever she can. Especially with the kids and any relationship they might have with *me*.
Gina I take it she's not with anyone.
Annie If only.
Gina (*lightly*) Don't you know a fella you could introduce her to?
Annie Don't think I haven't thought about it. So. Whether we will get married or not, I don't know. I just don't know.
Gina Still. Don't seem much point having a ring on your finger nowadays.
Annie Oh, I don't know.
Gina I tried it once. Never again.
Annie (*smiling*) That bad, was it?
Gina Depends how you rate getting beaten up every Friday night.
Annie Oh Christ—sorry.
Gina Truth is, I've forgotten what he looked like. He gave me a broken arm, a fractured skull and two kids I'd give my life for. I reckon I done all right out of it.

The cordless phone rings. Annie answers it

Annie Hallo? Oh, hallo, Dawn. ... Right. ... Right, that's fine. See you about quarter to—bye. (*She switches off the phone, sips her coffee*) Are you with anyone now?
Gina A bloke you mean? No.
Annie And you—cope, do you?
Gina Are we talking mentally, sexually or financially?
Annie (*smiling*) Money.
Gina Oh—money.

Annie Well ... on your own, two children to support...
Gina I manage very nicely, thank you.
Annie Sorry.
Gina No hand-outs, no begging bowls. What I've got I've worked for.

A moment

Annie Sorry.
Gina It's just that, a woman in my position, people assume. You're either on the take or you're available, you know what I mean?

A moment

Annie Yes. Yes, I do.
Gina I've got four houses like you I do a week and a pub I do Sunday mornings. A few other bits and pieces when I'm lucky. Enough to make sure my kids don't miss out. Cos the truth is, that's all I really care about. As long as I can give 'em a good start, a decent education. D'you know, when I first come to this area, after all the trouble—you know—I used to go around, looking at all the schools, trying to decide what would be the best for my two. I used to stand outside the gates, watching 'em going in and coming out—trying to get a picture, you know what I mean?
Annie Very sensible.
Gina Sensible—right. So one morning I'm at this school—North End Road—and this woman comes along and we start having a little chat and I tell her what I'm doing and she says you don't want to send 'em here, love, you should see the fights in the playground, the teachers can't pull 'em apart. But they're only five years old, I says. I'm not talking about the kids, she says, I'm talking about the mothers. No... I never thought I'd hear myself say it but I get enough money put away and my kids are going private. (*She finishes her coffee*) Thanks very much. (*She takes the mug to the sink*)

David comes in

David Where did we put the toolbox?
Annie In the cupboard.
David Course we did—thanks.

David goes into the walk-in cupboard

Gina All right if I do the bathroom?
Annie (*calling*) Have you finished in the bathroom?

Act II, Scene 1   47

David (*from the cupboard*) Me? Yes.
Annie Yes. (*She smiles*)

Gina goes out into the hall

Annie finishes her coffee and takes it to the sink as we hear the clink of tools being dropped

David (*from the cupboard*) Shit.
Annie What do you want the tools for?

David comes out of the cupboard, sucking a thumb, holding a hammer, screwdriver and pliers. He and Annie will scarcely make eye contact

David That window in the back bedroom—have we got any plasters?
Annie I thought you said the thingy had gone—let's have a look.

She looks at his injured thumb and goes to take a box of plasters from a drawer

David Sash cord. No, I think it's just slipped off the whatsit.
Annie Haven't you got an appointment?
David One o'clock.
Annie Here. (*She indicates for him to hold out his hand. She puts the plaster on for him*)

He catches her hand

David I shouldn't have said what I did, I'm sorry.
Annie No.
David I didn't mean all that stuff, you know I——
Annie It's just so pointless letting yourself——
David You're right, you're absolutely right, no excuses, I was out of order, completely out of order.
Annie He's an old man, I think he spends a lot of time on his own and I think he gets lonely.

A moment and he smiles

David Yeah.
Gina (*off; calling*) Hallo?
Annie (*at the door, calling*) Yes, Gina.
Gina (*off; calling*) Can you come up for a second?

Annie (*calling*) Right. (*She makes to go but stops*) I heard him crying.
David Crying?
Annie Last night. I was putting the chain on the door and I heard him crying.
David He was probably drunk.
Annie No—it wasn't that sort of crying. It was—I don't know, it was pitiful.

Annie goes out

He takes up the tools and makes to go out with them but looks at the party wall. He moves to it, putting his ear against it, listening. And then, under his breath, and with a cynical edge, he sings "Don't Cry For Me, Colonel Hewlett"

Scene 2

The sitting-room and hallway. Next day. Late afternoon

Hewlett stands, his back to us, looking out of the window. He turns, looks round the room absently, looks down at his open hands

After a moment Annie comes in from the kitchen, carrying a vase of roses

He visibly brightens on seeing her and her smile. She sets the vase down

Annie There.
Hewlett You do like roses, I hope.
Annie Love them.
Hewlett Slightly past their best, I'm afraid.
Annie No, no, they're lovely, really lovely.
Hewlett Although I must say I prefer them like this. Slightly—faded. Not so—garish—is that the word?
Annie It's *a* word, I'm not sure it's *the* word. (*Again the smile that he likes so much and she indicates for him to sit*)
Hewlett I think perhaps...
Annie No, no—please—unless there's something you...
Hewlett No, no. (*He smiles and sits neatly*)

She sits. Slight pause

The Elsmores said they could sometimes hear our clock. Through the wall. As loudly as if it were in the room he said.
Annie Yes.
Hewlett You hear it too, then.

Act II, Scene 2   49

Annie Sometimes.

A moment and then, despite himself and with a stiff attempt to make it sound jocular

Hewlett Just the clock I trust.
Annie Oh, yes, just the clock. (*She gives him her smile which seems to reassure him*) Does that mean you can hear us?
Hewlett The odd ... noise.
Annie You mean the odd—verbal exchange.
Hewlett (*smiling*) Something like that.
Annie What you should know about David and me is that he's an Aries and I'm a Leo which means we're both very opinionated and so a lot of, um, "discussion" goes on—quite unnecessarily because I'm always right and he's always wrong. Anyway, I'll try to make sure we keep it at a reasonable level.
Hewlett Not on my account, please.
Annie Of course on your account. (*She smiles*)

Another awkward moment

Can I get you anything? Tea or something?
Hewlett Absolutely not. Thank you.

Again a pause. She attempts to lighten it

Annie As long as your wife doesn't think I'm stealing you away.
Hewlett Sorry?
Annie Your wife—I'm sorry I don't know her name.
Hewlett Kristina—ah—yes—I see what you mean. Ha. No, she's, er, she's at her art class. She goes to an art class.
Annie Locally?
Hewlett At the community centre.
Annie I must ask her about it.
Hewlett You, er, you paint, do you?
Annie Not for years—but I was saying to David, I'd really like to start again.
Hewlett Ah.

Another pause

Deirdra—my—first wife—was really rather good. She made figures. (*He demonstrates a small figure*)
Annie In clay.
Hewlett Clay, yes. Clay. (*And he says what he's been wanting to say*) It's

five years ago to the day that she died. I've been to the cemetery. I took her some of the roses, she loved roses. Well, as you can see from our garden.
Annie It's a beautiful garden.
Hewlett I do my best but she was the one with the, with the really green fingers. (*He smiles*) Five years ago today.
Annie Had she been ill long?
Hewlett We'd known for about—four months. That's the thing, isn't it? You have no idea and then ... she died like she did everything else: very quietly and with the minimum of fuss. Almost her last words to me were instructions about food and clothing. I'm rather inclined to—take it as it comes, you see. D'you know ... a few weeks after she died, I looked into our freezer—we have this ridiculously large freezer—and she'd left all these little packages for me—meals she'd made up. All neatly packaged and labelled so that... I'm sorry.
Annie Not at all.
Hewlett Very presumptuous of me.
Annie Why presumptuous?
Hewlett My dear lady, I scarcely know you and here I am...
Annie I'm flattered that you trust me.
Hewlett Trust you.
Annie Isn't that what you're doing?

A moment

Hewlett Yes. Yes, I think it is. (*He tries a smile*) Annie... (*He clearly wants to say something to her, but can't*)

As he is shaking his head, the front door opens and David comes in wearing a jacket and tie and carrying a wrapped bunch of freesias and a newspaper

David Hallo?
Annie In here. (*She moves quickly out into the hallway*) Anthony's here, he brought me some... (*And she sees that David is holding flowers. She takes them, gives him a kiss*)

Hewlett stands up

Freesias. My favourite. I'll put them in water. (*She gives him a look saying "take it easy"*)

He answers with a "now would I not?" shrug

Annie goes into the kitchen as David moves into the sitting-room, rubbing his hands breezily

Act II, Scene 2   51

David Anthony—how nice to see you. (*He tosses down the newspaper and "notices" the flowers. Over-largely*) Roses ... you brought her roses.
Hewlett From my garden, yes.
David How nice, how very very nice. Please. (*He means sit. He himself sits untidily, loosens his tie*)

Hewlett sits. David smiles, deliberately maintains a silence

Hewlett You've not had any more trouble with your car, have you?
David How d'you mean more trouble? Sorry.
Hewlett It starts all right, does it?
David On the button. Why do you ask?
Hewlett There was an AA Breakdown chappie here this morning. Someone's car wouldn't start—chap from the college. Turns out that some idiot had stuck a potato up his exhaust pipe.
David Well, I never.
Hewlett Restricts the flow of gases, apparently, and the whole shoot goes phut.
David Does it really?
Hewlett As I say, obviously some sort of idiotic vandal so I'd check before you start the engine if I were you.
David Oh, I will, I will. (*He "beams"*)

Annie comes in with the freesias in a vase

Annie Will what?
David I'll tell you later.
Annie (*of the flowers*) My lucky day.
David That's the thing about flowers, isn't it? You can wait weeks for a bunch and then all of a sudden two come along at the same time.
Annie (*lightly*) D'you know, I think he's jealous.
David I cannot deny it.
Annie That's what he's like, you see, Anthony: insanely jealous.
Hewlett Of me? Ha!
Annie Of anyone. But you in particular.
Hewlett I wish.
David You old goat, Anthony. I do apologise—that's not offensive, is it?

Annie looks at him. For all his promising, it looks like he can't resist taking a potshot

   Anyway: as long as your wife's not jealous.
Annie I said the same thing.

David Oh?
Annie Anthony bringing me flowers.
David Oh—right. Right. When are we going to meet her, by the way?
Hewlett Yes, I...
David Tell you what—how about this evening? We've got nothing on, have we, Annie? This evening, yeah, that would be good.
Hewlett Unfortunately my wife is away.

Which slightly surprises Annie

David Still away?
Hewlett Unfortunately yes.
David Oh, well—when she gets back then.
Hewlett Yes, that would be... (*But he stands up*) Thank you for your hospitality. Good evening. (*He gives a curt nod to David and goes to the door*)

Annie follows him. During the following, David takes up the newspaper

Annie Goodbye, Anthony. And thank you for the roses, they're lovely.

Hewlett smiles and makes to go

Hewlett I wasn't always a hesitant old fool, you know. There was a time I was so certain about everything. So sure. Good night.

Hewlett goes out

She closes the door after him, goes back into the sitting-room

David There you are, you see—good as gold.
Annie Mmm. (*She kisses the top of his head*)

He catches her hand in his, draws her down and kisses her on the mouth. A longish kiss

> You're a good kisser, I'll give you that. (*She takes the newspaper from him and moves to sit and will flip through the paper*)

David All my women say that.
Annie Not all of them, surely?
David (*grinning, stretching, hands behind head*) It's all down to my first girlfriend, Frances Waye.
Annie Thanks ever so much, Frances, we're ever so grateful, we really are.

Act II, Scene 2   53

David I took her out one night and that weekend I happened to take a quick look at her diary...
Annie Happened to take a quick look...
David She used to keep this diary—you know what girls are like at that age.
Annie Twenty-seven you mean.
David Fourteen.
Annie Fourteen—oh, yeah, absolutely.
David "Thursday. Went out with D. F. Rotten kisser". I was destroyed.
Annie Makes a change.
David Luckily my friend Brendan Learoyd had this book: "How to Kiss, Price Twelve and a Half P".
Annie (*looking at him directly for the first time*) You're kidding.
David 'S true. What you had to do was cut an orange in half and...
Annie I don't think I want to know, thank you. (*She lowers the paper*) What d'you fancy for supper?
David What is there?
Annie There's the rest of the chicken. I could make a salad.
David How about if I did my pasta?
Annie D'you want to?
David Certainly. (*He gets up breezily and moves to the door*)
Annie What were you going to tell me?
David Tell you?
Annie You were talking to Anthony and I came back and you said——
David It was nothing really—just him going on as usual. (*He makes to go*)
Annie David ... you know I said I think he gets lonely...
David You know, I really thought we might have an evening without...
Annie I'm sorry—you're right—go and make your pasta. (*She takes up the paper*)

He stands for a moment then moves back to sit on the arm of her chair

David (*gently*) Let's have it then.

A moment

Annie I think he's trying to tell us something. Well, to be honest, tell *me* something.
David Like what?
Annie I don't know. I don't know.
David So you're saying you don't think he keeps knocking on the door because he's lonely but because he's got something he wants to tell you.
Annie Both, I think.
David He's got a wife, Annie.

Annie Come on, David.
David OK, OK, maybe he can't talk to her.
Annie Or maybe it's *about* her.
David He can't talk to *her* so he talks to his next door neighbour—someone he's known for, oh, nearly three weeks.
Annie I know, I know. It's just...
David Intuition. With me, it's paranoia. With *you*... (*He shrugs exaggeratedly*)
Annie Her name's Kristina by the way.
David Oh ... he's told you that much, has he?
Annie Yes ... he's very—guarded about her, I'll give you that.
David Well, he's certainly not in a rush to show her off. Not that she's ever here by the sound of it. Maybe it's as simple as that: it was a mistake, they don't get on. I mean she is half his age—sorry to mention it, *but*.
Annie Maybe. Anyway, from the way he talks I think anyone would have a job measuring up to his first wife. He obviously adored her. That's probably why I heard him crying: today is the anniversary of the day she died. (*She reaches up to touch his face briefly*) Go on—go and make your pasta.

He kisses her brow lightly and moves to the door but stops

David I wish I could feel sorry for him, Annie, but I can't. There's just something... I dunno.

David goes into the kitchen

Annie takes up the paper to read again. But can't. She puts it down and gets up to follow him out. She pauses at the roses. She bends, cupping a rose in her hand to smell it. And the petals separate, fluttering from her fingers to the floor. We bring up the sound of the ticking clock

SCENE 3

The kitchen/breakfast room. The following Friday. Morning

Gina, wearing a tight lowcut top and jeans, is spray-polishing and wiping down the counter tops

David comes in, in shirtsleeves, using the cordless phone

David Entering the kitchen now... (*To Gina*) Annie says is there anything you want?

Act II, Scene 3

Gina We could do with some bleach—that's about it.
David Bleach. ... No, just bleach. ... Me? No, thanks—yes—you could pop into Buy And Queue and get me some shelf brackets. I'm gonna put some shelves up in the kitchen cupboard. ... Yeah, I know but we could do with some more. ... Err ... good point, you're absolutely right ... leave it, I'll get 'em myself. Yeah. Yeah. Love you too. (*He puts down the phone and, whistling cheerily under his breath, goes into the cupboard, switching on the light so that the cupboard lights up. He pokes around in the toolbox*) I won't be disturbing you, will I?
Gina I'll let you know.
David Where's that bloody ... ah, there you are. (*He pulls out a tape measure, measures the width of the shelfless wall near the top*) Eighty-six... (*He measures the wall lower down*) And ... eighty-four and a half. (*He re-measures them both*) Eighty-six ... and eighty-four and a half. Right. Good. (*He whistles his way out of the cupboard to take up a pencil and paper*) So that's four times ... what did I say?
Gina Eighty-six and eighty-four and a half.
David Thank you. (*He writes, then goes back into the cupboard and measures the width of the existing shelving*) Twenty. Right. (*He regards the work in hand*) Did Ike put these shelves up?

A slight moment. She seems unsure of how to answer

Gina I think he did, yeah.
David (*not heavily*) I wonder why he didn't go all the way round.
Gina Dunno. P'raps he ran out of wood.

He taps the shelfless wall at about its centre. He realizes it sounds hollow and taps again, firmer

David That's why, he probably couldn't get a fixing.
Gina Yeah?

He taps the wall again, this time to the left and right hand sides

David (*more to himself*) It's all right here... (*He taps the centre area again*) it's this bit. Sounds like there's nothing behind it. I'll have to get some of those special waddaya-call-'ems.
Gina Wall plugs.
David Wall plugs.
Gina Cavity wall plugs.

He comes out

David "Cavity" wall plugs. (*He raises his eyebrows, "impressed"*)
Gina When I haven't got a good magazine I read a builder's catalogue and when I haven't got a builder's catalogue I read a sauce bottle.
David The things you learn about people. (*He takes up the pencil again*)
Gina Isn't that a fact?
David What did I say?
Gina Twenty.
David Twenty. (*He sits and writes up his list of requirements for the job, whistling under his breath again. He finishes, and sits, thinking ahead to the task, absently watching Gina. But becomes aware of her sexuality and finds himself enjoying her movement*)

She becomes aware of his eyes on her. He smiles broadly, breaking the mood. She goes back to her counter polishing

Gina (*not loudly*) Bugger.
David What's happened?

She bends to pick something up

Gina My necklace. The catch keeps slipping.
David Let's have a look.
Gina No, it's all right.
David (*moving to her, holding out his hand*) No, no, let me have a look.

She gives him the necklace. He looks at it, fiddles with it

   It's a nice chain.
Gina I think so.
David Present from an admirer?
Gina My kids. They saved up for months.
David Try it now.
Gina What have you done?
David The little lever was bent—try it now.

She takes the necklace from him, puts it round her neck. Doing so swells her breasts. She fumbles with the catch

   Here, let me do it.

And before she can stop him, he is gently turning her and their hands touch as he takes the clasp of the necklace from her. She stands as he closes the clasp

   There. (*He doesn't take his hands from her neck for a moment*)

Act II, Scene 3   57

Gina Thank you. (*She moves away from him to go back to her work*)

He stands for a moment, not sure if he hasn't got a little too touchy-feely, and then he moves away, brightly changing the subject

David Something I've been meaning to ask you.
Gina Oh, yeah?
David First time you came here you said... he can be a funny old devil. Next door. The Colonel.
Gina Did I?
David I wondered if there was any special reason. For saying that.
Gina Like what?
David Like... I dunno. I just assumed...
Gina I don't know much about him. Other than what Ike told me.
David Which was just him being a bit ... peculiar.
Gina He's getting on a bit. People get older they sometimes get a bit funny, yeah?
David Annie says people just get more like they always were.
Gina She must really look forward to growing old with *you*, then.

He grins. But is unnerved, not quite knowing what she means

David We still haven't met his wife.
Gina No?
David She's always away.
Gina Is that right?

Slight pause

David Although we're... (*he flutters a hand*) getting a picture.
Gina Yeah?
David Not from him. My friend Mr Shivraj the newsagent. Apparently she's—er—not what you'd expect. Which is more or less what you said.
Gina Don't think so.
David Implied, then.
Gina If you say so.

A moment

David (*lightly*) I get the feeling I'm in your way.
Gina Your house. You want it cleaned, I have to work. (*She looks at him directly*) No offence.

A moment

David (*standing up*) Right. (*He makes to go out*)
Gina Just one thing... he was a great bloke, Ike... but he had his dodgy side.
David How d'you mean?
Gina Just that. He was a bit dodgy. A bit light on his feet. A bit of a chancer. Especially when his wife wasn't around. Like a lot of men in my experience. (*She holds her look at him, raising her eyebrows as if to say "you take my point"*)

A moment. And David goes out

She finishes her polishing, then moves to the table ... and sees that the cupboard door is still open. She moves to it. Stands looking inside and then moves in. She stands looking at the shelfless wall and, after a moment, raises a hand as though to knock on it. But stops herself. She comes out of the cupboard and closes the door

SCENE 4

The sitting-room and hallway. The next morning

Annie is putting a table lamp on a newly-acquired side table. She stands back and assesses it, doesn't like it and starts changing the position of the table and the lamp

The front door opens and David comes in

David Annie?
Annie (*bad-tempered*) What?

He pockets one key and quietly puts a second key on the hallway shelf and goes into the sitting-room

David Sounds like you're having a good time.

She remains with her back to him, glowering at the table lamp

Annie If I put it here the wire doesn't reach.
David So put it at the other end. (*He moves up behind her*)
Annie I don't like it at the other end.
David (*putting his arms around her waist*) So I'll make it longer. (*He kisses the back of her neck and moves to look out of the front window*)
Annie Anyway. I'm not sure I like it here.

Act II, Scene 4

David Whatever. I'm going to have a shower.
Annie Where've you been?
David Paying the paper bill. I said.
Annie You've been ages.
David There was a queue.
Annie In the newsagents?
David It's Saturday. Everyone's paying their bill.
Annie Oh, yeah? (*She turns to look at him*)
David Yeah.
Annie It's a good job I love you.
David Why now?
Annie Don't ask.
David You love everyone.
Annie Correct.
David So what's so special about me?

She falls back into an easy chair

Annie You're a wonderful lover.
David Apart from that.
Annie There is no apart from that and on second thoughts you're not that good.
David Seriously.
Annie Oh, stop playing with yourself and go and have your shower.
David Whatever you say, madam.

She gets up and moves the table and lamp back to its original position

I thought we might go to that bathroom shop, have a look at some tiles.
Annie Yes. (*She smiles at him*)
David Then we could go down to that pub by the river.
Annie Mmm.

He moves away, looks at the bookshelves

David You haven't seen that Siegfried Sassoon, have you? The war diaries.
Annie Didn't I see you with it upstairs?
David I thought I put it back.

He continues to look through the books

Annie I know what I meant to tell you: Gina rang.
David Oh?

Annie She might have to give in her notice.

Slight pause

David Why's that?
Annie Apparently she's been offered another job at a lot more money.
David Is that all she said?
Annie More or less.
David She could have told you when she's next in.
Annie She wanted to warn me—give me more chance to find someone else I suppose.
David You don't think she's trying it on, do you?
Annie How do you mean?
David You know—trying to push up her money.
Annie I shouldn't think so for one minute. (*She somewhat irritably moves the table and lamp back to the other position*)
David She—er—she's very sharp.
Annie Yes and she's very honest. She says something, I believe her. Anyway. it isn't certain. She'll let me know on Monday. You're up to something, aren't you, you've got that shifty look.

Which indeed he has, guilty that Gina might have said something about his behaviour earlier

David (*deflecting her*) Yes, all right, Miss Marple, I've been shooting the breeze with my friend Mr Shivraj.
Annie Gossiping like two old women.
David D'you want to hear what he said or not?
Annie No. Go on, then.
David About six months ago, Colonel Whisky was in the local paper.
Annie If you mean Anthony say Anthony.
David Anthony.
Annie How d'you mean, in the local paper?
David I love it. He was out in the street waving a gun about and someone called the police.
Annie Anthony?
David Anthony. Apparently the corner house across the road was empty and he was convinced there were squatters trying to get in so he goes out into the street in the middle of the night—blind drunk apparently, and waving this gun about.
Annie What happened?
David Bound over to keep the peace.
Annie Anthony?

David Anthony.

Slight pause

Annie Is that it?
David Well, you've got to admit it's funny.
Annie Hysterical.
David You know what I mean, Annie.
Annie No other little titbits?
David You really want to know?
Annie I really want to know.
David All right: he's cancelled all her magazines.
Annie Whose magazines?
David Next door. Apparently *Anthony* went in and cancelled all his wife's magazines—she had about three a month apparently.
Annie Apparently, everything's apparently.
David Marie Clare—Cosmopolitan—stuff like that—and he cancelled the lot.
Annie She's away, why shouldn't he?
David He cancelled them permanently.
Annie So what are you trying to make out of that?
David Makes you wonder, that's all.
Annie No, it makes *you* wonder. Tell me: when you have these little chats with your friend Mr...
David Shivraj.
Annie Mr Shivraj, does he volunteer this stuff or do you squeeze it out of him—no, don't bother, I can work it out for myself and I thought you were having a shower?

He grins and goes to the door

David There's been talk about her and Ike.
Annie (*irritated*) Her who?
David Her next door. The Colonel's lady. Katrina. Mr Shivraj's son saw them sitting in a car one night—in the car park at the back of the cinema.

David goes out and upstairs

Annie stands for a moment. Thinking to herself, sod you, sod you, David, for putting these thoughts into my head

Annie (*calling half-heartedly*) You know you really...

She is interrupted by a polite knock at the front door. She sees a figure—

Hewlett—on the porch and ducks out of sight so that she herself cannot be seen. She waits. After a moment, a magazine is put through the letterbox. The figure moves away. She waits a moment and then moves to take up the magazine. She looks at it—it is a gardening magazine. She moves back into the sitting-room

Scene 5

The kitchen/breakfast room. The following Monday. Morning

David sits using his portable word processor and phone

David (*into the phone*) Two hundred. By the end of next week. That's a definite, is it? ... Great, I'll give you a number... fifteen seven seven oh eight. ... Cheers, Freddie. (*He rings off and taps information into the word processor. Then closes it down and stands, pulling on his jacket. As he does, he becomes aware of a noise from the party wall. He moves, still pulling on his jacket, closer to the wall. He listens*)

We bring up the sound of something being banged into, of someone— Hewlett—cursing drunkenly, then of a glass breaking. David moves away from the wall, jerking his head. Then has a thought. He takes up the phone. He has a second thought, but then, what the hell, he dials. And waits and, as he does, he pulls out his handkerchief and puts it over the mouthpiece

(*With a disguised voice*) Is that Mr Hewlett? This is British Telecom, good morning, sir, your wife has been enquiring about our Family And Friends discount scheme. ... Did you not, sir?

During the following, Gina comes in with some cleaning materials which she takes into the cupboard

Oh, I see. When will she be available? You're not sure. Well, what I'll do is give her a ring later in the week, thank you so much, sorry to have troubled you, goodbye.

He rings off and, when Gina comes out of the cupboard, uses the handkerchief to wipe his nose. He will be somewhat uneasy with her. Her attitude certainly seems a lot frostier than it did at their last encounter

Be out of your way in a second.

Gina Yeah, I've got to do the floor.

David Sorry. (*He collects up his work things*)

She runs her hands under the taps and dries them as he takes up a small pile of papers

Where shall I put these?
Gina What's that?
David Some old papers I want to chuck out.
Gina Leave 'em on the side, I'll put 'em in the bin.
David Thanks. (*He takes the papers to the counter, sorting through them as he goes, just to make sure he isn't throwing away anything important. He puts them on the counter*) Thanks. (*He makes to move away, but something on the top paper catches his eye and he takes it up. It is the estate agent's specification of the house—two pages stapled together. He glances through it*) That's what it was. (*He goes out into the garden, still holding the paper. We see him stand, looking up and along at the wall. Then he comes back in, opens the cupboard door, looks inside in confirmation*)
Gina Excuse me. Are you going to be here much longer because I want to get on.
David Sorry. Just, er, just something I remembered. (*He puts the paper in a drawer and takes up his computer and case and makes to go*) Annie says you've decided to stay on.
Gina Yeah.
David I'm glad. I mean I'd hate to think it was anything I'd—you know—I mean ... the last thing I'd want to happen is to have you—you know—misunderstand.
Gina I'm thick but I'm not stupid.

Slight pause. He tries to make light of it

David I'm not sure I know how to take that.
Gina Take it how you like.

A moment

David Bye, Gina.
Gina Have a nice day.

Another moment and David goes

She looks towards the door. Men. She puts the chairs on the table, ready to clean the floor. Is about to do so when, on impulse, goes to the drawer and takes out the piece of paper. She looks at it. Then she looks up and towards the cupboard

Scene 6

The sitting-room and hallway. Two days later. Evening

David and Hewlett sit, drinking wine. Both appear a little tipsy. David is in apparently ebullient mood

David (*replenishing Hewlett's glass*) I mean. Now you've planned it, you might as well execute it. That's if you really want to.
Hewlett If that's what you'd like, absolutely.
David I mean to be honest I'm hopeless at gardening and Annie isn't much better so having someone like you would be absolutely fantastic.
Hewlett Well, then.
David Absolutely bloody fantastic. (*He tips his glass to Hewlett*)

They drink. Or rather David pretends to drink, his eyes very much on Hewlett

So what will you do, come in as and when?
Hewlett A couple of times a week should do it.
David Perfect.
Hewlett This time of year of course there's not overmuch to do.
David If you say so.
Hewlett Then we're into the clearing up and preparation.
David Annie said something about vegetables.
Hewlett Why not?
David You know what I'd really like? Rhubarb.
Hewlett Rhubarb.
David Rhubarb. I love rhubarb. Rhubarb and custard.
Hewlett Jolly good.
David In my opinion, if more people eat rhubarb there'd be less trouble in the world.
Hewlett I never thought of that.
David People don't.
Hewlett Something in it, is there?
David The theory you mean.
Hewlett No, the rhubarb.
David I believe there is, yes: same stuff as there is in St Whatsits Wort. Very calming apparently.
Hewlett Keeps the bowels moving, I know that.
David Well, you couldn't ask for much more, could you, Colonel?
Hewlett Ha!

They drink. David tops up Hewlett's glass again

David (*all chums together*) Tell me ... is that right that Ike's wife was a bit of a madam.
Hewlett How d'you mean, madam?
David Well, all right, a bit of a cow.
Hewlett She was very—er—Australian.
David Right.
Hewlett Middle-class Australian. On the other hand, she was a Monarchist.
David Is that right—Ike was brought up in the bush with aborigines?
Hewlett So he was fond of saying, yes.
David Makes you wonder what they could have had in common—not him and the aborigines, him and his wife.
Hewlett He has a great deal of charm.
David And—and—certain women like a bit of rough, eh, Colonel.
Hewlett Do they?
David Oh, yes. Like my Annie. (*He winks and grins widely*)
Hewlett That I can't say.
David Take my word for it.
Hewlett When will she be back?
David Annie? Not long. She's gone to see her mother. She's very good like that. I said, didn't I—old people, children and animals. (*He "drinks"*) Oh, yes, they like the Ikes of this world. All that rough-diamond-hairy-chested-who-gives-a-toss charm of his, eh?
Hewlett I've no idea.
David He certainly turned it on for Annie.
Hewlett Oh, yes?
David Oh, yes. Mind you, I've no doubt he turns it on for all of them. I'm sure your wife must have had the benefit.

Hewlett doesn't answer

Eh?
Hewlett Again—I've no idea.
David I understand she's a very attractive woman.
Hewlett I would say so yes.
David Bound to, then.
Hewlett D'you mind if we talk about something else?
David Oh. Sore point. Sorry.
Hewlett Not a sore point at all. I'd just rather...
David Absolutely.

Silence

I know what I've been meaning to ask you ... did they take it away?

Hewlett Take what away?
David Sorry—your gun. Presumably it was a memento from your army days.

A moment

Hewlett Did who take it away?
David The police. That night you were—you know.

A moment

Hewlett It was confiscated and then returned.
David You've got a licence then, have you?
Hewlett It had been disarmed.
David Oh, *I see*. So you couldn't really have shot those squatters even if you'd wanted to.
Hewlett Where did you hear all this?
David (*shrugging*) Just talking.
Hewlett I had no intention of shooting anyone.
David Just wanted to frighten them.
Hewlett It was very stupid of me.
David You stuck your head up over the parapet though, didn't you? Most people would have sent for someone else to do the dirty work.
Hewlett They were breaking into private property.
David That's what I mean. Tell me: what would have happened if they'd turned nasty?

Hewlett looks at him, then finishes his wine and stands

Hewlett I think I should go now. Thank you for your hospitality.
David (*standing*) No—really—I'd like to know—what would you have done?

Slight pause

Hewlett I don't understand the question.
David Well you were taking a helluva chance, weren't you? I mean, there you are, a man of a certain age, "having a go", waving a gun about, what if they'd found out it was useless, just a bit of window dressing—and decided to have a got at *you* instead?
Hewlett The thought never occurred to me.
David Mind you ... the Parachute Regiment ... you must have been well capable of looking after yourself. Still are for all I know. (*He grins*)

Hewlett I was—well capable, as you say.
David So what would you have done?
Hewlett I really don't...
David I'm interested, I really am.
Hewlett I would have done what was necessary.
David Which was what?
Hewlett Mr Freedman...
David David. I'd really like to know. (*He advances on Hewlett, arms outstretched in mock attack*) Here's this bloke coming at you... twice your size... half your age... what would you do?

Suddenly Hewlett's hand shoots out and he is grasping David by the neck, applying pressure. David, taken completely by surprise and clearly helpless, is brought slowly down to his knees. Hewlett maintains his grip

Hewlett A little more pressure, Mr Freedman, and I could crush your oesophagus. Which means you would drown in your own blood. (*He releases his grip*)

David remains on his knees, getting the breath back into his lungs

That's what I would have done. That's how I would have defended myself. If necessary.

David slowly looks up at him

The front door opens and Annie comes in

Annie (*calling*) David? (*She tosses her keys onto the hall shelf and goes into the sitting-room*)

She sees David getting to his feet. She looks from him to Hewlett

David?
David It's all right, it's all right... Anthony was showing me how he—got his badge for unarmed combat.

She can only make the uneasy assumption that it has been some sort of silly game

Annie (*with a half-smile*) Is that right, Anthony?
Hewlett Yes. I was demonstrating to Mr Freedman—David—how easy it is to defend oneself when one's assailant has made the arrogant assumption

that one is much drunker than one actually is. (*He gives her his little smile*) A little game and nothing for you to worry about. (*He gives a curt nod to David*) Good-night. (*A nod to Annie and he goes out of the room*)

She is so confused that she momentarily forgets her manners ... and then goes out into the hallway after him

Annie Good night, Anthony.

Hewlett already has the front door open. He turns as though to say something, but changes his mind, smiles, and goes out

She closes the door and moves quickly back into the room where David is now sitting

David How was your mother?
Annie Doesn't matter about that, what the hell's going on? (*She pulls off her coat and tosses it over a chair*)
David We were having a drink. Fooling around.
Annie Fooling around? Him?
David I asked him to show me what would happen if——
Annie Why would you ask him in for a drink?
David To talk about the bloody garden.
Annie You can't stand the sight of him, you wouldn't ask him in for *that*.

He doesn't answer

  Would you? Would you?
David OK, I wanted to get him drunk. I wanted to see if I could make him ... say things.
Annie About what?
David About his wife.
Annie You're obsessed with the woman—why?

A moment

David Because I think he's killed her.

She can only look at him

Annie You think what? (*She has tried to make it sound like he's made a poor joke*)
David I know, I know, but...

Act II, Scene 6

Annie So tell the police. You think our next door neighbour has killed his wife, tell the police.
David I will, of course I will.
Annie (*hands spread*) Well?
David When I'm sure.
Annie (*dismissively*) Wonderful.
David Just sit down and listen to me. Please.
Annie I don't want listen to you...
David Just sit down and listen to me, just listen to what I've got to say. Please. Please.

A moment. She sits. He cranks himself up to start

>Every time we ask about her he makes an excuse about why she isn't here. No-one has seen her—and, yes, all right, I've been asking around—no-one has seen her since the beginning of last month.

Annie David.
David I've been inside the house. (*He knows exactly how she will react*)
Annie (*quietly*) You've what?
David I used their key and I went into their house.
Annie When?
David One afternoon when I saw him go out.
Annie You're obsessed.
David Listen to me, Annie...
Annie My God, you're...
David There's nothing of her there.
Annie What d'you mean, there's——
David No clothes, no possessions, nothing.
Annie (*all she can think to say*) She's gone away—on holiday.
David There's nothing *of* her, Annie. He sleeps in a single bed, in a single room, and there's no evidence of anyone else in the house. It's as though she doesn't exist.

A moment

Annie She could have left him.
David Yes.
Annie Taken everything and left him.
David Yes.
Annie Well, there you are then.
David Why doesn't he say so?
Annie Well, obviously, he's embarrassed.
David OK, so why does he keep coming into this house?

Annie He said why.
David All that stuff about forwarding letters, hearing burglars, d'you really believe all that?
Annie Of course I do.
David Annie ... he's been in here a lot more than you know.

A moment

Annie What?
David I knew he was coming in and out of here and so I—all right, I set a trap.
Annie You did what?
David I fixed it so that I would know if anyone had opened a door, you know, a bit of Sellotape, things like that.
Annie (*softly*) My God.
David He's been in here, Annie. In here, in the kitchen, upstairs...
Annie All right—why?
David I think two reasons. One, because of what happened here and two, because he's checking up, making sure we're not getting any closer.
Annie Closer to what?
David Closer to what's happened to her.

A moment

You think I'm off my rocker.
Annie Why? Why would he kill her?
David OK. He's seventy-something years old. His beloved wife has died and he's lonely. He meets a woman half his age and twice as cunning who sees him as a meal ticket. It happens all the time. They get married. Before you know it she's waving her legs in the air for——
Annie Just keep it simple, will you, David?
David Before you know it, she's having an affair with friend Ike. Maybe it started before his wife goes back to Australia, maybe after. Whatever. I reckon the Colonel knew about it and just turned the other cheek, hoping it would all straighten out when Ike went. But something happened. I don't know what ... maybe she started throwing it in his face or maybe it was something he heard in this house...

She tries to interject but he continues

Ike arranged for the phone to be kept on his account until the twenty-seventh, when we moved in. I got it about two weeks ago and sent it on as we'd arranged. But first I opened it. I don't know why, something made me open it. (*He takes papers from his pocket*) I made a copy of it. (*He holds it out to her*)

She looks at him in disgust

Look at it, Annie. Please.

A moment. And then she takes the papers and looks at them

Three calls have been made from this house to numbers in Australia *after* Ike moved out. They weren't made by me and they weren't made by you and I think they were made by the Colonel's lady. I think that whatever she was arranging with him, it was heard by the Colonel. Maybe they were just talking dirty, I don't know. But I think he came in here, probably drunk, confronts her, she throws it in his face, he loses his rag and kills her, probably not meaning to, but believe me he's quite capable of killing, he panics, hides the body, doesn't admit what he's done and so the longer he keeps it to himself the harder it is to confess ... and we turn up. A week earlier than he thought we would. Annie, I know it sounds crazy, but it happens. People do kill each other. Ordinary people. I mean for chrissake you read about it every day of the week.

Annie So what you're saying is—just let me get this right—what you're saying is he killed her and her body is somewhere in this house.

A moment

David Yes.
Annie He kills her and then comes in here and makes polite conversation.
David Because he can't *stop* coming in here. *Think* about it, Annie, put yourself in his shoes...
Annie And he's going to leave her here, is he?
David I don't know and I don't think *he* does.
Annie I see.
David He's done something, he's panicked, and it's all gone wrong. He's in a spiral and he can't control it. I dunno ... maybe he thinks he'll get rid of her when he's got time, when we go away or something ... maybe he's got it into his head to somehow blame Ike. I *dunno*.

She turns her head away from him, almost shivering at the thought, but

Annie All right. Where is she? In the garden? Yes, he's always going on about the garden...
David I don't think so.

Annie Where then? The cellar—no, hold on, we haven't got a cellar—the attic—is that where she is, the attic?

A moment

David I'll show you.

Hold this moment between them

Scene 7

The action is continuous into the kitchen/breakfast room

The Lights come on and David comes in, followed by Annie

Annie Well?

A moment. Then he moves to stand near the cupboard, indicating it

David You remember I was going to put up some more shelves in this cupboard.
Annie (*stiffly*) Something else you never quite got round to doing—yes?

He switches on the light so that the cupboard lights up and goes inside, pushing the door fully back so that she can see

David The reason I was having so much trouble is that part of the wall ... this bit here (*he taps the wall in different places, indicating the differing degress of solidity*) seems hollow, like there's nothing really solid behind it.
Annie I'm still listening.
David Then I realized that this wall ... didn't line up from the outside... I measured it. It's something like three feet smaller measured from the inside than from the outside. I didn't think too much of it at the time—I may have been way off with my measuring—I mean, I know I'm pretty clumsy with a tape measure in my hand ... but something kept nagging me, something I felt I ought to have remembered. (*He takes a folded paper from his pocket*) And then I was throwing out some old papers from when we bought the house and for some reason I looked at the agent's original specification and there it was... (*He unfolds the paper and gives it to her to read*)

She does so, unwillingly

Act II, Scene 7

(*Pointing it out*) "The kitchen contains a large walk-in cupboard and small cold room". Do you remember looking in this cupboard when we first saw the place?
Annie Vaguely. Yes. He just—opened the door and showed us. It was full of junk I remember.
David That's it—we just took a quick look—hey, a nice big cupboard—and moved on. And I suppose we were so pleased with the place that we didn't go back and analyse all the crap they put on paper. But this is what they mean, Annie. Behind this wall is a small cold room, an old pantry. This bit here ... would have been the door. It's had a thin panel put over it and been papered and painted to match the rest of the wall. And you can see by the paint that it was done recently. Why would anyone try to hide a door, Annie?

A moment

Annie You do know what you're telling me, don't you, David.
David I think she's in there. Yes. I think he killed her, put her in there, and walled her up. Ike left enough stuff to decorate an entire house. Timber, hardboard, paper, paint...
Annie Well, there's only one way to find out, isn't there?
David Annie.
Annie You've come this far, you can't back out now. So do it, David. Do it.
(*She remains standing by the garden door*)

A moment. He pulls off his jacket, tosses it over a chair, and opens up the toolbox which is on one of the shelves. He takes out a Stanley knife, goes to the wall and scores round the outline of the door. Annie remains where she is

At the same time, we begin to hear the sound of the ticking clock from next door. Quietly at first but gathering sound as David gets a finger hold and, with difficulty, peels back the nail-fastened panel, slowly revealing the old-fashioned panel door. He sets the panel to one side and turns his attention to the door itself. There is no handle. He pushes a screwdriver against the jamb and eases the door

The ticking of the clock is now at a crescendo as, not without trepidation, David puts his hands along the door edge and pulls at it ... there is no movement at first and then suddenly the door springs open, and as it does a long bundle falls out, making David jump back fearfully and in this moment, the loud ticking of the clock comes abruptly to an end

David stands, breathing heavily ... and realizes that the bundle at his feet is of timber and metal in a black plastic bag, tied with rope. He looks past it into the small dark space. Nothing there. He stands for a moment, then moves out of the cupboard ... and for the first time realizes that Annie has witnessed all this. Her face is enough to tell him

David You knew, didn't you?
Annie I wanted to see how far you'd go.
David You knew.
Annie Just before he put the house on the market, good old Ike discovered that your little "tomb" was riddled with woodworm. It could have meant arguing about the asking price and he didn't want that, he wanted a quick sale and off to Oz, so he spent an afternoon with his do-it-yourself kit. Gina tried to tell you he wasn't quite the trust-me-I'm-your-best-friend bloke he made out to be.
David So she told *you*, all girls together.
Annie Once you started making a thing out of it, yes. Otherwise she would have let us find out for ourselves. She liked Ike. For all he was light on his feet.

A moment

David And you let me...
Annie I said. I wanted to see how far you'd let the poison eat into you.
David Poison?
Annie You can't let go, David. It's a poison.
David You've humiliated me.
Annie In whose eyes, David? (*She holds her look at him and makes to go in to the hallway*)
David This isn't to say he hasn't killed her.

She stops

Annie No. Well ... only one way to find out the truth, isn't there, you'll have to ask him. Or better still, why don't you do what you always do—leave it to me?

Annie gives him a flat smile and goes out

He stands watching her. Then he turns and moves back into the cupboard. He remains staring at the dark space within

Scene 8

The sitting-room and hallway. The next day. Late morning

Hewlett is with Annie

Hewlett (*taking an opened letter from his pocket*) As it happens... I had a letter from her this morning. (*He offers the letter to her*)

She indicates that she doesn't want to see it. He takes the letter out of its envelope and glances at it

She's in Melbourne.
Annie With Ike.
Hewlett Oh, yes. With "Ike". He had no intention of going back to his wife it seems. How long my wife's—"charms"—will continue to excite him, I've no idea.
Annie I'm sorry.
Hewlett My dear lady. (*After a moment*) I first met her when she looked after Deirdra. She was a nurse, you know. She seemed so very kind and—understanding. Some time after Deirdra died, she called at the house. To see how I was. (*He gives a sardonic little jerk of the head*) And things... took their course. She was very efficient in all departments—including the finances. Especially the finances. She will have done very well for her—services. I certainly should have seen what was going on between them in this house. Truth is, he all but told me. "Ike". He has no style, you see, no class. He couldn't resist—boasting of his conquests but... none so blind. And then I came home one day to find a note—four or five lines I think it was—to say she'd left me and I sat down and I had a couple of whiskies and then a couple more and I thought of what a complete fool I'd made of myself with this—this—"woman"—and I lost control I suppose and I went around the house, taking up everything of hers I could find, getting rid of any trace of her, throwing it away, burning it. It was very stupid of me and afterwards I felt deeply ashamed. And I couldn't tell anyone, you see. I couldn't face the—the what? The ridicule, I suppose. And I found I couldn't keep out of this house, that I needed to come in here and—feed off the contempt I felt—feel—for myself. (*He has lost himself in the telling of this story, but now snaps out of it and looks directly at her and tries his smile*) No fool like an old fool.
Annie No page that can't be turned.
Hewlett Yes. Yes.

They smile at each other and then he stands up

I told your husband—I told David that I'd make a start on your garden this morning.
Annie Are you sure you——
Hewlett We agreed.

A slight moment

Annie Well, then.
Hewlett I'll just, err... (*He indicates go through*)
Annie Yes.

Hewlett looks at her and goes out, along the hallway and into the kitchen

Annie moves to look out of the (unseen) french windows into the garden

After a moment, the front door opens and David comes in, carrying a loaded B & Q bag. He comes into the sitting-room

She glances round to see him and then turns back to look out of the window. There is clearly a tension between them. A moment

David OK?
Annie Fine.

A moment

David (*trying to make it sound light, jokey even*) I, umm, I thought I ought to do something about that cupboard. I've got some, er, I've got some woodworm stuff.
Annie (*flatly*) Yes, why don't you? (*She moves to the door*) Oh, and I think you're right. I think we might have rushed things. I think we don't look far enough ahead, either of us. I think maybe we've got a lot more talking to do.

Annie holds her look and then goes out and up the stairs

He stands, poleaxed. He moves to the door

David Annie? (*He remains standing, then moves slowly back into the room, to stand looking out of the front window*)

Hewlett comes through from the kitchen

Hewlett Ah. You're back.
David (*miles away*) What?

Act II, Scene 8

Hewlett I'm starting on the garden. I wondered if you still want the old pear tree pruned.
David Oh. Yes. Whatever. (*He turns and offers a humourless smile*)

Annie appears coming down the stairs, buttoning on a cardigan. She sees Hewlett

Annie I thought I'd give you a hand.
Hewlett I'd enjoy that.
Annie So would I.

Annie smiles at him and goes into the kitchen

Hewlett Will you be joining us?
David No no. You go and—enjoy yourselves.

Hewlett nods and moves to the door

Hewlett Old soldiers never die. They only live next door. What? What? (*He smiles. A happier smile than we have ever seen from him*)

Hewlett is even whistling as he "toddles off" after Annie

David is left alone. He sits, not knowing quite what to do

Gina comes in through the front door

He turns to see her as she passes on her way to the kitchen

Gina (*brightly*) Hi.
David How are you?
Gina Great. My boy's birthday today.

Gina gives him a happy smile and continues into the kitchen

He stands for a moment. The phone rings. He takes it up

David (*flatly*) Hallo? ... Oh—Ike—yeah—how are you?

From outside the sound of Annie's laughter

(*Turning to look out of the french windows, the phone at his ear*) Yeah, we are. Everything's great. Great. Great.

Curtain

FURNITURE AND PROPERTY LIST

Further dressing may be added at the director's discretion

ACT I

Scene 1

On stage: Sitting-room/Hallway:
    Carpet
    Curtains part-drawn across two of three windows
    Large sofa
    Boxed-in radiator; its top serving as window seat
    Radiator, its top serving as shelf. *On it*: 3 or 4 letters
    Empty book shelves
    2 marble fireplaces
    2 cardboard boxes containing books and ornaments
    3 paintings stacked against wall
    Phone
    Front door chain

Off stage: Cardboard box full of odds and ends (**David**)
    Bottle of champagne, 2 glasses (**Annie**)
    Glass, ugly beaker (**David**)

Personal: **Annie:** piece of paper
    Hewlett: key, neat little pad, pen

Scene 2

On stage: Kitchen/Breakfast Room:
    Walk-in cupboard containing shelving, toolbox
    Unpacked boxes
    Cordless phone
    2 mugs of coffee
    Cooking utensils

Off stage: Box full of bits and pieces (**David**)

Furniture and Property List

Personal: **Gina:** thin gold necklace (worn throughout)

SCENE 3

On stage: SITTING-ROOM/HALLWAY

Set: Small Edwardian cushioned chair
2 table lamps
Books on shelves
Pictures
Low steps

Off stage: Minimal food shopping (**Annie**)
Card (**Hewlett**)
Newspaper (**SM**)

SCENE 4

On stage: KITCHEN/BREAKFAST ROOM

Set: Table. *On it*: 2 cardboard boxes
3 empty boxes near french windows
Chairs
Radio
Towel
Load of crockery
Annie's shoulder bag containing work diary

Off stage: Cordless phone (**Annie**)

SCENE 5

On stage: SITTING-ROOM/HALLWAY

Off stage: Large glass of water (**David**)

Personal: **Hewlett:** 2 keys

SCENE 6

On stage: KITCHEN/BREAKFAST ROOM

Set: Laptop computer
David's jacket

	Mug of coffee
	Sheet of paper
	Pen
	Towel
Off stage:	Full wastebasket (**Gina**)
Personal:	**David:** key

Scene 7

On stage:	SITTING-ROOM/HALLWAY
Set:	Bottle of red wine
	2 wine glasses
	Pad
	Pen
Off stage:	Briefcase (**David**)
	Glass (**David**)
Personal:	**David:** car keys

ACT II

Scene 1

On stage:	KITCHEN/BREAKFAST ROOM
Set:	2 coffee mugs
	Hammer, screwdriver and pliers in cupboard
	Box of plasters in drawer

Scene 2

On stage:	SITTING-ROOM/HALLWAY
Off stage:	Vase of roses (**Annie**)
	Wrapped bunch of freesias, newspaper (**David**)
	Freesias in vase (**Annie**)

Furniture and Property List

SCENE 3

On stage: KITCHEN/BREAKFAST ROOM

Set: Spray-polish
Dish cloth
Toolbox
Tape measure
Pencil
Paper

Off stage: Cordless phone (**David**)

SCENE 4

On stage: SITTING-ROOM/HALLWAY

Set: Side table. *On it*: table lamp
Easy chair

Off stage: 2 keys (**David**)
Gardening magazine (**SM**)

SCENE 5

On stage: KITCHEN/BREAKFAST ROOM

Set: Laptop computer
Phone
David's jacket
Small pile of papers

Personal: **David:** handkerchief

SCENE 6

On stage: SITTING-ROOM/HALLWAY

Set: 2 glasses
Bottle of wine

Personal: **Annie:** keys
David: papers

Scene 7

On stage: KITCHEN/BREAKFAST ROOM

Set: Toolbox on one of cupboard shelves, containing Stanley knife and screwdriver
Nail-fastened panel
Long bundle in black plastic bag, tied with rope

Personal: **David:** folded paper

Scene 8

On stage: SITTING-ROOM/HALLWAY

Off stage: Loaded B & Q bag (**David**)

Personal: **Hewlett:** opened letter

LIGHTING PLOT

Practical fittings required: table lamps, cupboard light
2 interiors

ACT I, SCENE 1

To open: Early afternoon late summer lighting on sitting-room and hallway

No cues

ACT I, SCENE 2

To open: Afternoon lighting on kitchen/breakfast room

No cues

ACT I, SCENE 3

To open: Early afternoon lighting on sitting-room and hallway

No cues

ACT I, SCENE 4

To open: Morning lighting on kitchen/breakfast room

Cue 1   **Gina** turns on cupboard lights   (Page 30)
        Snap on cupboard light

ACT I, SCENE 5

To open: Street lamps shining through front door

Cue 2	**David** switches on main light *Snap on sitting-room light*	(Page 30)
Cue 3	**Annie** switches on side lights, switches off main light *Snap side lights and switch off overhead light*	(Page 30)

ACT I, SCENE 6

To open: Morning lighting on kitchen/breakfast room

No cues

ACT I, SCENE 7

To open: Evening lighting on sitting-room and hallway

No cues

ACT II, SCENE 1

To open: Mid-morning lighting on kitchen/breakfast room

No cues

ACT II, SCENE 2

To open: Late afternoon lighting on sitting-room and hallway

No cues

ACT II, SCENE 3

To open: Morning lighting on kitchen/breakfast room

Cue 4	**David** switches on cupboard light *Snap on cupboard light*	(Page 55)

Lighting Plot

ACT II, SCENE 4

To open: Morning lighting on sitting-room and hallway

No cues

ACT II, SCENE 5

To open: Morning lighting on kitchen/breakfast room

No cues

ACT II, SCENE 6

To open: Evening lighting on sitting-room and hallway

No cues

ACT II, SCENE 7

To open: Evening lighting on kitchen/breakfast room

Cue 5   **David** switches cupboard on light   (Page 72)
            Snap on cupboard light

ACT II, SCENE 8

To open: Late morning lighting on sitting-room and hallway

No cues

EFFECTS PLOT

ACT I

Cue 1	**David** kisses **Annie** on cheek *Car horn sounds, brief but irritable*	(Page 2)
Cue 2	**David** exits *After few moments, ticking of grandfather clock, growing louder*	(Page 15)
Cue 3	**Annie** starts unpacking box *Phone rings*	(Page 19)
Cue 4	Outline of figure appears at front door *Doorbell rings*	(Page 22)
Cue 5	To open Scene 4 *Radio playing pop music, not loudly*	(Page 28)
Cue 6	**Annie** switches off radio *Cut radio music*	(Page 28)
Cue 7	**Gina** comes out of cupboard *Sound of clock ticking next door*	(Page 28)
Cue 8	**Gina** turns on radio and turns up volume of music *Bring up radio music*	(Page 30)
Cue 9	To open Scene 5 *Ticking of grandfather clock, fade as* **David** *and* **Annie** *arrive*	(Page 30)
Cue 10	**Annie**: "David…" *Phone rings*	(Page 32)
Cue 11	**David**: "…I'm pissed off." *Front doorbell rings*	(Page 34)

Effects Plot

Cue 12	**Annie** climbs stairs *Ticking of grandfather clock*	(Page 37)
Cue 13	**Gina**: "I saw Annie before she left." *Phone rings*	(Page 38)
Cue 14	**Annie**: "He's just … being nice." *Sound of a car alarm, off, not over-loud but insistent*	(Page 43)
Cue 15	**Annie** sits, looking straight ahead *After a moment, cut car alarm; after a moment's silence, bring up ticking of grandfather clock*	(Page 44)

ACT II

Cue 16	**Gina**: "I reckon I done all right out of it." *Cordless phone rings*	(Page 45)
Cue 17	Rose petals droop at **Annie**'s touch *Ticking of grandfather clock*	(Page 54)
Cue 18	**David** listens close to wall *Bring up sound of something being banged into, of someone—**Hewlett**—cursing drunkenly, then of a glass breaking*	(Page 62)
Cue 19	**David** scores round outline of door inside cupboard *Bring up ticking of grandfather clock from next door, quietly at first but gathering sound*	(Page 73)
Cue 20	**David** eases door ready to open it *Bring ticking of clock to crescendo*	(Page 73)
Cue 21	**David** jumps back from released bundle *Cut ticking of clock*	(Page 73)
Cue 22	**Gina** exits into kitchen *After pause, phone rings*	(Page 77)

www.ingramcontent.com/pod-product-compliance
Ingram Content Group UK Ltd.
Pitfield, Milton Keynes, MK11 3LW, UK
UKHW021844210426
53221PUK00022B/453